SUCCESS STORIES of IAS Exam CRACKERS

RAKESH KHAIRWA, DANICS

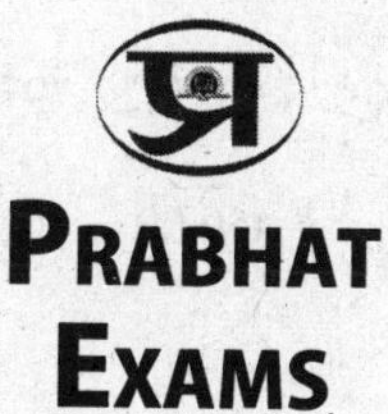

PRABHAT EXAMS

Publisher

PRABHAT EXAMS

Imprint of Prabhat Prakashan Pvt. Ltd.

4/19 Asaf Ali Road, New Delhi–110 002

Ph. 23289555 • 23289666 • 23289777 • Helpline/ 7827007777

e-mail: prabhatbooks@gmail.com • Website: www.prabhatexam.com

Price

Four Hundred Fifty Rupees

ISBN 978-93-5322-797-5

Printed at

Sita Fine Arts, Delhi

SUCCESS STORIES OF IAS EXAM CRACKERS

by RAKESH KHAIRWA, DANICS

ISBN 978-93-5322-797-5

₹ 450.00

कर्मण्येवाधिकारस्ते मा फलेषु कदाचन ।

मा कर्मफलहेतुर्भुर्मा ते संगोऽस्त्वकर्मणि ॥

भावार्थ : तेरा कर्म करने में ही अधिकार है, उसके फलों में कभी नहीं। इसलिए तू कर्मों के फल का हेतु मत हो तथा तेरी कर्म न करने में भी आसक्ति न हो॥ 47॥

-भगवद गीता :- अध्याय-**2**, श्लोक-**47**

मन में अथाह शक्ति है। मन ये शक्ति कहाँ से लाया ? परमात्मा से ! जैसे सूर्य और उसकी किरण, जैसे सागर और उसकी तरंग, जैसे टॉर्च और उसका प्रकाश, ऐसे ही परमात्मा और मन । अगर आप अपने मन को एकाग्र करके किसी लक्ष्य के ऊपर केंद्रित करते हैं तो दुनिया में ऐसी कोई वस्तु नहीं है जिसे आप प्राप्त ना कर सकें।

सिविल सर्विसेज परीक्षा में हर वर्ष अनेक ऐसे अभ्यर्थियों ने इस परीक्षा को पास किया है जो प्रारंभिक परीक्षा होने तक अपने वैकल्पिक विषय को भी ठीक तरीके से नहीं पढ़ पाए थे परंतु उन्होंने टेस्ट सीरीज के माध्यम से, अपनी लेखनी तथा निरंतर अभ्यास के द्वारा परीक्षा से संबंधित टाइम मैनेजमेंट का पालन करते हुए अंतिम रूप से चयनित हो गए। इसलिए सकारात्मक रहते हुए मेहनत करें। आपको सफलता अवश्य मिलेगी ।

Dr. B.M. MISHRA, IAS
District Magistrate (South)

Office of the District Magistrate (South)
Govt. of N.C.T. of Delhi
M.B. Road, Saket, New Delhi-110068
Off. : 011-29535025
Email : dcsouth@nic.in

D.O. No. DC/South/2019/308

Dated : 21/10/2019

Dear Sh. Rakesh,

It is with great pride and joy that I offer you my heartiest congratulations for this unique compilation. I firmly believe that proper guidance for UPSC exams is paramount for any aspirant especially for the one who resides in rural area.

It takes tremendous hard work and proper guidance to qualify prestigious UPSC Civil Services Examination.

Each and every page of this book is the journey of successful candidates with diverse educational backgrounds belonging to various parts of the country. Many of them had faced arduous and unpropitious situations in their life in general and particularly during preparation phase even though many had to face economic hardship as well but one thing is common to all that they had immense faith in their capabilities and faculties.

Some journeys are exceptional. Unique thing about this compilation is each successful candidate has penned down her/ his journey in own words. This aspect makes the book very interesting and depicts a real picture.

With his voracious and laudable efforts, Shri Rakesh Khairwa, a DANICS Officer presently posted as SDM, Saket at New Delhi has compiled all the information about selected candidates, their journey while preparing for the examination and success mantras shared by them which are very useful for all UPSC aspirants.

I extend my sincere gratitude to Mr. Rakesh for his commitment and dedication. Further, I am fully confident that these success stories will inspire many young graduates for choosing Civil Services as a career option and will keep motivating them during their preparation phase and service life.

I wish a successful career to the selected candidates in Civil Services.

With Best Wishes,

21/10/19

(Dr. B.M. Mishra, IAS)

Sh. Rakesh Khairwa, DANICS
SDM (Saket), South Delhi

Preface

Dear friends,

This book is an outcome of sheer hard work of successful candidates. Previously, I had given thought to publish the success stories last year too but it could not materialize. Subsequently, when I came in contact with successful candidates, I realized that some had so unique journeys that I could not resist myself to give shape to the idea which was in mind since long. Again, the question arose to whom should I approach since I had known only limited number of successful candidates.

Through social media and with the help of friends, I could collect stories of 58 successful candidates of 2018 Civil Services Examinations. I would like to thank to all officers who manage their time to write their story since many of them have joined the services and some were re-appearing for improvement in rank.

While preparing for this examination our mindset is not same at all the times. Sometime we feel highly motivated, sometime energy and motivation level is very low when prelims, mains or final result has announced especially when result is not as we expected. Through this book, you will come to know that many candidates did not give up, prepared relentlessly and finally made it to the selection list. Some stories are extremely motivational so as to make you realize that yes you can also make it. Just always be positive.

As written by many officers that there is no substitute of hard work and dedication. Further, let me make clear here that I could not collect data from southern states due to my own limitations. I hope in next version it will be more balanced and comprehensive.

I wish to thank to almighty, my parents, family members, my wife Poonam, daughter Sanvi and son Bhavya for their constant support and all my friends who contributed their time and energy for this, without their support it would have not been possible. I will grateful to all of you for this unique opportunity. I would like to thank Piyush ji of *Prabhat Prakashan* who got ready to publish this compilation enthusiastically in one call.

In this book you will find a unique success pattern of each successful officer. Some of them come from backward areas, some have average educational qualification, so that you may realize that successful candidates not born with a silver spoon. Some of them were already in job, it is interesting to see how they could sale through their arduous journey and made it to the destination.

There are many books available in market but this compilation is unique. While going through each story, I firmly believe that you will find stories among top 10 itself that will provide you immense hope and will keep you constantly motivated throughout your own journey. I will be honored to have suggestions from your side also for additional inputs for improvement and pointing out correction or any suggestion ; you may mail us at rakeshkhairwa001@gmail.com.

Further, I wish to announce here that I have not added anything from my side in this book, it is simply a compilation. All stories are provided by CSE 2018 officers themselves. I extend my sincere gratitude to all the successful candidates who manage their time to provide their success story and wish them successful career in Civil Services.

With best wishes.

Rakesh Khairwa

Contents

Preface.. *vii-viii*

S.NO.	NAME	RANK	PAGE NO.
1.	Kanishak Kataria	1	1-6
2.	Shubham Gupta	6	7-10
3.	Vaishali Singh	8	11-13
4.	Ankita Choudhary	14	14-16
5.	Anuraj Jain	24	17-21
6.	Garima Agrawal	40	22-25
7.	Vikram Grewal	51	26-29
8.	Sumit Kumar Rai	54	30-33
9.	Manisha Rana	67	34-35
10.	Dilip Pratap Singh Shekhawat	72	36-46
11.	Pradeep Kumar Dwivedi	74	47-50
12.	Jay Shivani	81	51-54
13.	Nidhi Siwach	83	55-59
14.	Abhishek Jain	111	60-61
15.	Atul Kumar Bansal	115	62-67
16.	Manish Meena	144	68-71
17.	Dr. Pooja Gupta	147	72-73
18.	Ram Niwas Bugalia	159	74-76
19.	Dipankar Choudhary	166	77-79
20.	Arpit Bohra	178	80-82
21.	Siddhartha Nahar	182	83-86
22.	Hanul Choudhary	191	87-89
23.	Maninder Singh	195	90-95
24.	Akshay Kabra	207	96-100
25.	Kunal Aggarwal	211	101-104

26.	Pankaj Lamba	236	105-107
27.	Manjeet Singh	256	108-110
28.	Inderveer Singh	259	111-113
29.	Anju	272	114-116
30.	Anshul Jain	285	117-119
31.	Vasudha Sehrawat	310	120-121
32.	Aditya Kumar Jha	339	122-124
33.	Prateek Bayal	340	125-127
34.	Natisha Mathur	351	128-130
35.	Tarun Tomar	374	131-133
36.	Yashraj Nain	382	134-135
37.	Garima Dahiya	394	136-138
38.	Hitesh Kumar Meena	417	139-140
39.	Anil Kumar Jhajharia	431	141-142
40.	Satyanarayan Prajapat	445	143-146
41.	Lokesh Yadav	452	147-149
42.	Vikas Marmat	473	150-152
43.	Hemant Kumar Meena	532	153-155
44.	Sparsh Gupta	562	156-159
45.	Jagdish Kumar	564	160-162
46.	Devender Singh Chaudhary	575	163-166
47.	Rahul Kumar Singh	579	167-173
48.	Rajendra Chaudhary	590	174-176
49.	Krishan Kumar Poonia	632	177-178
50.	Mintu Lal Meena	664	179-180
51.	Sachin Kumar	669	181-182
52.	Dinesh Kumar Meena	678	183-185
53.	Hemant Singh	679	186-188
54.	Pawan Kumar Meena	702	189-191
55.	Devender Prakash Meena	705	192-195
56.	Vijendra Kumar Meena	707	196-198
57.	Satender Singh	714	199-203
58.	Jyoti Meena	741	204-205

1

Name: Kanishak Kataria
Rank: 01, CSE-2018

Stay optimistic throughout your journey and believe in yourself. My pillars of success are 'optimism, hard work, and self-confidence'.

KANISHAK KATARIA

OPTIONAL SUBJECT
Mathematics

MEDIUM
English

NATIVE PLACE
Jaipur, Rajasthan

EDUCATIONAL QUALIFICATION
- B.Tech with Honours in Computer Science and Engineering, IIT Bombay – 2014

PARENTS' OCCUPATION
- **Father:** IAS Officer, Rajasthan
- **Mother:** Homemaker

COACHING TAKEN
- GS – Vajiram and Ravi, Delhi
- Mathematics – IMS, Delhi

MARKS
Prelims: Paper -1: 106 and Paper -2: 147.5

MAINS MARKS AND PERSONALITY TEST
Essay (Paper I): 133
General Studies- I (Paper II): 098
General Studies- II (Paper III): 117
General Studies- III (Paper IV): 117
General Studies- IV (Paper V): 116
Optional - I (Mathematics) (Paper VI): 170
Optional - II (Mathematics) (Paper VII): 191
Written Total: 942
Personality Test: 179
Final Total: 1121

MY JOURNEY

- Most of my schooling was done in Kota, Rajasthan, a city well known for its IIT and NEET (then PMT) coaching's. Being good in Mathematics and having an aptitude for Science, I naturally got attracted to engineering (and IITs) for graduation.
- I appeared for the IIT-JEE examination in 2010 and secured AIR 44. I opted for IIT Bombay for its all-round career options and Computer Science as my branch because of my interest in the subject plus the opportunities which were present in the sector.
- My father had recommended UPSC as a career option to me right since my childhood. After my graduation in 2014, he again asked me to appear in the UPSC examination. However, I always wanted to explore multiple options before making such a pivotal decision in my life. I had secured a job offer from Samsung Electronics, South Korea. It was an amazing opportunity for me to get exposure outside India and also explore the private sector - an offer which I accepted.
- I moved back to India in 2016 and started working in a private firm in Bengaluru. Although UPSC was an option always lingering in the back of my mind, I never gave a serious thought into it during this period (September 2014 - April 2016).
- It was only after I had spent 7-8 months in Bengaluru that I started contemplating more seriously about my career. Comparing my life outside India and then in India, I felt there is much work that needs to be done in India and as an individual, I can also contribute towards it.
- Having seen my father work, I was aware that if I join administration, I could create a more meaningful impact. Civil Services provides one with an opportunity to work in a diverse set of fields and be more satisfied with the work that one does.

- I discussed with a few officers with similar background about their experiences in administration and asked them if it would be a better career choice for me. I also got an opportunity to work in the US for a couple of months and later got a Masters admit from a US university (in April 2017). But my experiences abroad made it clear to me that I want to stay and work in India. Instead of preparing half-hearted heartedly, I preferred to first make it clear in my mind as to why I wanted to prepare for UPSC and after nearly 5-6 months of deliberation, I finally decided to prepare for UPSC.
- I had heard about the uncertainty and difficulty of UPSC. Moreover being away from studies, especially humanities subjects, I was aware of the challenge I was throwing myself into. However, I had clarity as to why I want to appear in UPSC and this challenge didn't feel that big. In fact, I was excited to learn more about subjects like History and Polity. Also, I decided to give only 2 attempts. If it was meant to be, I would clear the exam in 2 attempts and if not, I would move on from it.
- In May 2017, I quit my job to fully focus on UPSC examination attempt. I moved to Jaipur and started researching what and how I needed to prepare. I read a few blogs of toppers to see what needs to be done and then fixed the target for appearing in Prelims 2018.
- One of the 1st tasks I did was to finalise my optional as many toppers had focused a lot on its importance. I went with my strength, chose Mathematics as my optional and decided to make it my main-pillar (or X-Factor) in my preparation. After researching a little, I set a target of scoring above 350 in Mathematics. I knew if I score 350+ in optional, I would easily get into the IAS.
- In the meantime, I got in touch with a couple of my batch-mates from IITB (Bombay), who were also starting their preparation for UPSC. At the start, I was apprehensive about moving to New Delhi for preparation (as I liked to study alone in the comfort of my home). But in the company of my friends, I decided to move to New Delhi and join coaching so that my preparation could be streamlined. Given I had only 2 attempts in mind, I tried to find ways to maximise my returns in the 1st attempt itself.
- In June 2017, I shifted to New Delhi and joined Vajiram and Ravi for year long GS coaching for Prelims-cum-Mains and IMS for Mathematics coaching.

- In the initial 4 months, my full focus was on finishing the optional syllabus and have a basic minimum coverage of GS along with daily current affairs from newspapers. By October 2017, I finished 90% of my optional and then shifted fully on GS preparation.
- My GS preparation was always Mains oriented. I read the syllabus, saw previous years' UPSC questions and prepared for each subject accordingly, using a minimal resource list comprising of NCERTs, a single standard book, and coaching notes. For 2.5 months, my full focus was on GS and current affairs.
- In January and February 2018, I decided to revise my optional one last time before focusing fully on Prelims preparation, which I started in March 2018.
- In April 2018, I shifted back to Jaipur after the classes got over and started self studies. During March-May 2018, I prepared solely for Prelims (to be held on 3 June, 2018).
- After the prelims, I took a week's rest and then started my main preparation. For 1 month until the result of prelims was out, I focused on revising my optional and refining my answer-writing skills. I knew whether I clear the prelims or not, this phase was very important for overall preparation and focused on maximising my efforts.
- After the prelims result were out, I started revising my GS subjects and appeared in a test series (8 full-length tests). I focused more on revision instead of picking up new sources to read.
- The Mains finished on 7 October, 2018 and I decided to take a month's rest. I stayed in touch with the current affairs through daily newspaper reading. Post my GS papers, I wasn't confident about my performance and result. But I knew the optional was my X-factor and I was a little upbeat after a good optional paper in Mains. So my overall feeling was quite positive about the Mains' result.
- After the results for Mains were out (on 20 December, 2018), I started my Personality Test preparation. I appeared in a few mocks and prepared my DAF thoroughly.
- The Personality Test was scheduled for 6th March, 2019. After the PT, even though I tried to focus on Prelims 2019, I couldn't do so because of anxiety and curiosity about the result. There were mixed feelings - I had a hunch that if everything works as per my plan, I would clear the

examination but at the same time, I wasn't sure about my GS marks. Having appeared in Mains for the 1st time, there wasn't any surety of the marks given, the paper is subjective.

- It was 5th April, 2019 when the final results came out and I was shocked and a little relieved to have cleared the examination in my 1st attempt and get into IAS. AIR (All India Ranking) 1 was just a cherry on top of the cake for me. To be honest, I still haven't processed or realised the magnitude of that achievement yet. I am just happy to see the positive returns of my 1.5 years of hard work and having realised my dream in the very first attempt.
- The final result showed me that if the desire is real, motivation strong, accompanied by consistent hard-work, then everything falls into place. The examination might be considered one of the toughest to crack, especially in the 1st attempt but impossible is nothing. And it's just not me, there are multiple first attempters to have cleared this examination.
- Hopefully, in years to come more and more people would be able to realise their dream of clearing this examination with the minimal number of attempts.
- The last few months have been quite relaxing - I fulfilled the promise I made to myself at the start of my preparation and went on a month's travel. After that, I have been just relaxing at home and awaiting the start of training at LBSNAA (Lal Bahadur Shastri National Academy of Administration). To be honest I haven't seen many pics of the academy or training process which many previous toppers have shared. I wanted to keep my LBSNAA experience completely new and that's what excites me a lot about it!
- In the future lies the start of something new and challenging. I hope to undergo a wonderful training process and then get on with the work. Hopefully, I will pass the test and meet the expectations of everyone - me, my parents, my family and the people of this country - as an administrator.

MESSAGE FOR NEWCOMERS

- You have made a lot of sacrifices to prepare for this examination. If not someone else, just be true to yourself and remember why you want to come into civil services. More than subject knowledge, UPSC tests the psychology and emotions of aspirants a lot. If you are clear in your head, nothing can stop you from cracking UPSC.

- Do not fall into the trap of fear-instillers and rumour-mongers. Believe in yourself and your hard-work. People will say a lot of negative things like it can't be done in the 1st attempt but they all just want to bring you down. This exam is perfectly doable in one attempt. You just need to be a little strategic and smart with your studies. It does require a little bit of luck on the way but it only comes to your way if you have worked hard.
- Be consistent and do not reduce the intensity. Go hard in the initial 4 and last 4 months and save energy in the middle. Treat it like a marathon. If you prepare well in the first 4 months and finish your optional early, you are all sorted for the mains preparation.
- Do not worry about going to New Delhi or joining any coaching. In present-day and age, there are ample resources available online. If you can study well in the comfort of your home, believe me, there is no other place where you can prepare better!
- Be ruthless with your resources and habits. If something is not working just discard it. It something is working, do it again and again. Be less emotional and more mechanical.
- Do not compete with anyone else, your competition is with yourself. If you can improve daily and be a better version of yourself every day, it means you are heading in the right direction.
- Stay optimistic throughout your journey and believe in yourself. My pillars of success are 'optimism, hard work, and self-confidence'. In any moment of despair, they pulled me out of it and kept me going. Make them your armour and you can shield yourself from all negative thoughts and challenges.
- Keep limited resources. In the 1st attempt, it is nearly impossible to read each and every resource. Keep a clear focused strategy that suits you. Do not mimic someone else. If you see a topper has read 5 books, you also need to keep in mind the number of attempts he/she took for reading those many books. Guidance is needed but be critical and filter out those opinions which do not apply to yourself.
- At last, I would just tell you that UPSC is not everything in life. Open yourself to the outside world and see what opportunities lie in front of you. Do not focus on the result, instead, just enjoy the process. Even if you do not clear this exam, you are going to learn a lot and become a better person. Just live in the present, focus less on the results and do not think far ahead in the future. If you do so, you will get the result you deserve.

❑❑

2

Name: Shubham Gupta
Rank: 06, CSE-2018

Dedication, Commitment and Perseverance, the trinity of these three words is the formula for success in this exam. Have faith in yourself and you will definitely ace the examination.

SHUBHAM GUPTA

OPTIONAL SUBJECT
Law

MEDIUM
English

NATIVE PLACE
Bhudoli, Neem Ka Thana, Dist. Sikar (Rajasthan)

EDUCATIONAL QUALIFICATION
❖ B.A. (Hons.) Economics from Delhi College of Arts and Commerce, University of Delhi (2015)

PARENTS' OCCUPATION
❖ **Father:** Businessman ❖ **Mother:** Homemaker

COACHING TAKEN
❖ GS – Nirvana IAS ❖ Law – Nirvana IAS

MARKS
Prelims: Paper -1: 108 and **Paper -2:** 150

MAINS MARKS AND PERSONALITY TEST
Essay (Paper I): 139
General Studies- I (Paper II): 097
General Studies- II (Paper III): 124
General Studies- III (Paper IV): 101
General Studies- IV (Paper V): 118
Optional - (Law) (Paper I): 149❖ **Optional - (Law) (Paper II):** 155
Written Total: 883 ❖ **Personality Test:** 184 ❖ **Final Total:** 1067

CONTACT OPTIONS
Facebook:https://m.facebook.com/shubham1108.gupta
Instagram:https://www.instagram.com/shubhamgupta1108
Twitter:https://twitter.com/AskShubhamGupta
Blog:https://myantardhwani.blogspot.com

MY JOURNEY

- The journey for UPSC started at a very early age for me, sometime around when I was in Class V. My father, being a businessman, had a few bad experiences with the bureaucrats in his life. So, one day, he asked me to take up the challenge of becoming a 'Collector' so that I am able to provide the desired atmosphere to people who come to interact with the bureaucrats regarding various aspects related to their lives. This is when it struck a chord somewhere in my mind and took shape in the form of attempting the UPSC CSE during the formative years of my life.
- During this journey, I faced a lot of failures. It was a journey where not only I lost out professionally on achieving the desired outcomes due to reasons which were hard for me to decipher afterwards, but also where it was a personal loss as well where I lost out on friends as well as the close contact with my family. This was because every time I attempted the exam, either I was in college or I was under training which reduced the spare time that might be available for personal relationships. So much so, I can feel the loss even today!
- In 2015, I gave my first attempt in the CSE. I wasn't able to pass the preliminary exam. This was just after my graduation. I realized that I wasn't very well prepared in terms of the depth of knowledge required for the exam as well as the time management skills that were essential for success in this exam. Correcting these two flaws in my strategy, I ended up clearing the preliminary exam in 2016, followed by mains and subsequently I scored AIR (All India Ranking) 366 in that year. I was allocated the Indian Audit and Accounts Service. When I had a look at the mark sheet, I was shocked to see that my mains' score was amongst the top 5 rankers for that year but I had scored a paltry 124 in the Personality test. This really troubled me, I tried to analyze and identify my mistakes but wasn't able to single out flaws equivalent to deserving such a low score. My family also wasn't very enthusiastic about my preference for Indian Audit and Accounts Service over the Indian Revenue Service.
- Hence, I decided to take the plunge again and wrote the exam for the 3rd time. Lack of time and motivation proved to be a deterrent for me again and I failed the preliminary exam. This was a really disappointing turn of events for me especially since I was already in the services. However, it

made me realize the unpredictable nature of the exam. Meanwhile, my training for the Indian Audit and Accounts Service started in Shimla. It was essentially pretty tediously structured training wherein the classes were long enough from 9:30 in the morning to 5:30 in the evening followed by weekly treks on Saturdays. Hence, there was very limited time for me to prepare for the exam while training in Shimla.

- After a lot of contemplation, I decided to try my luck for the 4th time and probably the last time. I used to squeeze time out of my day after the classes and also tried to balance my love for playing various sports along with the need to study hard for the CSE exam. As luck would have it, I was one of the 3 people out of 16 of my batchmates who cleared the preliminary exam in 2018. This was followed by clearing the mains as well. Then came the stage of the Personality test where I had fared pretty badly the last time. Hence, I decided to give it my all this time and prepared really well. On the day, dressed in a blue suit, I sat in the waiting hall for almost 3 hours waiting for my turn. It was really hard for me to handle the butterflies in my stomach especially because of my past experience. I struggled to deal with it all and finished the test ultimately.
- On the result day, I had almost lost all hope that the results will be out that day. Suddenly two of my colleagues came running towards me shouting the fact that I had scored AIR 6 in the exam. I could not believe them and wanted to see the result with my own eyes. I was overwhelmed! The first thought that came to my mind was this that the 5 year old has finally been able to achieve what he aspired for so many years back. Even though it took time and a lot of hard work, the fruits were sweeter than expected. The whole world around me had changed overnight. People knew me; they wanted to talk to me. But I calmed myself down and told myself that this is not the end of the journey, but just the beginning.

MESSAGE FOR NEWCOMERS

- Dedication, Commitment and Perseverance. The trinity of these three words is the formula for success in this exam. In the preparation for UPSC, it's very important that one is completely dedicated to the preparation in the true sense, it should come from within and reflect in his 'antardhwani' or the inner drumbeat. This should be followed by commitment to the end result that one is trying to achieve by the way of clearing this exam and entering civil services. During this journey, it's equally important that the aspirant has faith in himself as well as the process so that he/she doesn't get bogged down by the baggage of failures and is able to pick himself/herself up every single time. It needs to be remembered that the nature of the exam is such that the best of the best gets humbled here. Hence, the process of constant learning is highly significant and increases your chances of clearing this exam manifold.

- For the aspirants, I would also suggest them to treat UPSC as just one of the stages of life and don't allow it to dominate all spheres of your life. UPSC is only a means to an end, and not the end in itself.
- As far as preparation is considered, I would like to advice the aspirants to stay organic in their preparation. Try to avoid referring multiple sources for one single subject and focus more on qualitative learning. Have faith in yourself and you will definitely ace the examination.

❑❑

3

Name: Vaishali Singh
Rank: 8, CSE-2018

'Identify your strengths and weaknesses and work on them. We must remember that we are stronger than we think and that we will get rewarded for our courage in some way or the other'.

VAISHALI SINGH

OPTIONAL SUBJECT
Law

MEDIUM
English

NATIVE PLACE
Faridabad (Haryana)

EDUCATIONAL QUALIFICATION
❖ BA.LLB (Hons.) – 2016

PARENTS' OCCUPATION
❖ **Father:** Lawyer
❖ **Mother:** Lawyer

COACHING TAKEN
❖ GS – Vision IAS

MARKS
Prelims: Paper -1: 122.66 and **Paper -2:** 124.18

MAINS MARKS AND PERSONALITY TEST
Essay (Paper I): 146
General Studies- I (Paper II): 103
General Studies- II (Paper III): 102
General Studies- III (Paper IV): 111
General Studies- IV (Paper V): 111
Optional - (Law) (Paper I): 151
Optional - (Law) (Paper II): 147
Interview: 195
Final Total: 1066

CONTACT OPTIONS
*Instagram: @_singhvaishali_*

MY JOURNEY

Ups and Downs and how to deal with them: Hello everyone! My name is Vaishali Singh and I have secured All India Rank 8 in Civil Services Examination 2018. Like everyone else, I too am a girl with a lot of dreams and finally my dream to become an IAS officer has come true. As I was inspired by the stories of others, I hope my story also inspires others.

I come from Faridabad in Haryana and did my schooling from Delhi Public School, Faridabad. As both my parents are lawyers, law as a profession became a natural choice for me. So after school, I decided to study law and did BA.LLB. (Hons) from National Law University Delhi. Certain experiences at law school, especially my work with IDIA (Increasing Diversity by Increasing Access to Legal Education) in my final year motivated me to go for a service like the civil services. However, as I had already received a job offer from a law firm till then, I decided to go for it to make an informed choice. After a few months, I quit my job as I decided to appear for the Civil Services Examination.

I started my preparation around January 2017 and decided to take law subject as my optional. I had only 5-6 months to prepare for my first attempt and I decided to go for it. I could not clear prelims by 5 marks in that attempt and was heartbroken. However 10 days after the result I analysed my mistakes. While I did gain good amount of knowledge for my first attempt, what was lacking was a good strategy. So for my second attempt, I focused on strategy a lot.

I did self study for my second attempt and focused on a few things: (1) Keeping my sources limited; (2) regular newspaper reading; (3) enough mock test practice. I learnt from my previous attempt that it was necessary for me to take regular breaks and to not miss out on things I like. So I travelled regularly and met my friends at regular intervals. While this one year journey was smooth, I faced certain unexpected challenges during both my Prelims and Mains. Due to a certain emergency, I could not study for nearly 15 days in the month of May- right before my prelims. My entire study flow broke. I somehow picked myself up in the last 10 days and brought my preparation back on track by doing back to back mock tests.

Similarly during mains, 2 days before my Optional Paper, I injured myself and got a ligament tear in my right wrist. My doctor advised to not move my hand at all and he wasn't even sure if I would be able to write for 6 hours on

2 consecutive days. I was finding it extremely difficult to write because it was very painful. However at that moment I just told myself that I cannot let my hardwork go waste and that the pain does not matter. What matters is that I have this opportunity to write the mains examination and that I will face this challenge irrespective of the situation. So I took a number of painkillers on the day of the exam, kept applying 'volini' spray on my hand while writing and I somehow managed to not only finish my exam but also score well.

So from these 2 experiences I learnt that we often face unexpected problems and difficulties during the most crucial days of our lives. But we can gather the strength to face it, so we must not panic. We must remember that we are stronger than we think and that we will get rewarded for our courage in some way or the other.

MESSAGE FOR NEWCOMERS

My message for the newcomers and the current aspirants is very simple – have faith in yourself and your capabilities. Identify your strengths and weaknesses and work on them. Both knowledge and strategy is important for this exam so try and understand the demands of this examination by looking at the past year papers – that's half the battle. Just work hard, be true to yourself during the preparation and take breaks as you need to be your best you!

LIST OF BOOKS

So I read very basic books and kept my sources very limited:

- MIH – Spectrum
- **Art and Culture** – Nitin Singhania
- **Ancient and Medieval** – Tamil Nadu Textbook
- **Polity** – Laxmikant
- **Environment** – Unacademy videos + some chapters from Shankar IAS book
- **Geography** – Class XI and XII NCERTs + G.C. Leong
- **Other mains topics** – made notes from information available online

❑❑

4

Name: Ankita Choudhary
Rank: 14, CSE-2018

Everyone of us has some or the other problems in life, some personal, some professional but the goal of becoming an IAS officer is worth giving everything in the form of hard work and consistency.

ANKITA CHOUDHARY

OPTIONAL SUBJECT
Public Administration

MEDIUM
English

NATIVE PLACE
Meham (Rohtak) Haryana

EDUCATIONAL QUALIFICATION
- Bsc Chemistry – Hindu College (DU)
  Msc Chemistry – IIT, Delhi

PARENTS' OCCUPATION
- **Father:** Record Keeper, Sugar Mill Meham

COACHING TAKEN
- GS – Vajiram
- Optional – Synergy

MARKS
Prelims: Paper -1: 122

MAINS MARKS AND PERSONALITY TEST
Essay (Paper I): 137
General Studies- I (Paper II): 97
General Studies- II (Paper III): 115
General Studies- III (Paper IV): 105
General Studies- IV (Paper V): 111
Optional - (Pub. Ad.) (Paper I): 163
Optional - (Pub. Ad.) (Paper II): 151
Interview: 182

MY JOURNEY

UPSC Examination is a lengthy process and if you are entering into the process, it is very important that one is mentally prepared for the challenges. It requires a lot of hard work and patience during preparation. For me, it was my second attempt in which I cleared, so I know my struggle is not very long but I can still suggest some dos and don'ts.

To keep yourself motivated during preparation phase is very challenging. So it is very important that you are determined to achieve your goal. You should not rest until your aim is achieved. Try to learn from your failures because failures are bound to be a part of your journey. Analyse your mistakes, look for your strengths as well as your weaknesses. Try to be optimistic.

Personally, my toughest challenge was my failure in the first attempt. But I didn't sit back. I went back to my preparation and I told myself that I could do it. It is very important that you believe in yourself. At that time, I wanted to boost my confidence therefore I applied for other jobs as well and that kept me focussed during the complete year.

The preparation is a continuous process, therefore, it is very important that one avoids taking long breaks. Try to study daily. Give yourself monthly targets on daily basis and try to achieve them. That boosts confidence. Prepare a time-table and do take small breaks in between to relax your mind.

I studied for approximately 10-11 hrs daily and I used social media as well as internet. I know people suggest to avoid social media but I would advise to have contacts with friends. It has helped me to relieve stress and tension but yes one can definitely avoid spending too much time.

Internet is a very useful source of information therefore I would advice everyone to prepare current affairs' notes from online sources like GKTODAY, INSIGHTS, PIB. Keep checking official sites of the government for latest information. Try to keep your study material limited. It is very important you revise your notes multiple times instead of referring to multiple sources.

We all a have a misconception that UPSC is for very intelligent people, toppers and all but what I have personally felt is that it is a game of multiple qualities like hardwork, patience, optimism, leadership. Therefore even if you are an average student, you can excel in these papers with proper strategies. Every one of us has a different strategy and different methoods have worked for different people so please make your own unique strategy. Try not to copy others' writing style, keep it real and unique.

For interview, try to keep yourself calm. The board checks your personality so it is very important you put your strong foot in front.

At last, I want to say that every one of us has some or the other problem in life, some personal, some professional. But the goal of becoming an IAS officer is worth giving everything in the form of hard work and consistency. Leave everything behind and just be focussed on your goal. Never get scared of failures in life. Take them as challenges. Fall and rise again.

❑❑

5

Name: Anuraj Jain
Rank: AIR-24, CSE-2018

When you have an internal motivation and a burning desire to succeed, then only you can sustain in this journey.

ANURAJ JAIN

OPTIONAL SUBJECT
Psychology

MEDIUM
English

NATIVE PLACE
Lucknow

EDUCATIONAL QUALIFICATION
- B. E (Hons) Electrical and Electronics & M.Sc (Hons), Mathematics BITS Pilani

PARENTS' OCCUPATION
- **Father:** Father is a businessman and mother is a homemaker

COACHING TAKEN
- GS – Joined Vajiram but largely missed classes due to excessive spoon feeding. Attended classes of Polity. Economics etc. Psychology: Pathak sir at Vajiram and Ravi.

MARKS
Prelims: 136

MAINS MARKS AND PERSONALITY TEST
Essay (Paper I): 100
General Studies- I (Paper II): 108
General Studies- II (Paper III): 115
General Studies- III (Paper IV): 113
General Studies- IV (Paper V): 116
Optional - (Psychology) (Paper I): 159
Optional - (Psychology) (Paper II): 174
Written Total: 885
Interview: 171
Final Total: 1056

MY JOURNEY OF UPSC

(a) Struggle

In the first attempt I had missed the final cutoff by mere 5 marks.

Then how did I improve between my 2 attempts?

In my second attempt, I had identified the areas where I had to work upon having a decent scope for improvement. I had following targets in mind

Essay can be improved by 35 marks (going by marking of CSE 2017)

Psychology could give a bump of around 30-35 marks

General Studies overall had a good score, yet again 20 marks could be an improvement (going by marking of CSE 2017)

Interview could give a final edge by 5-10 marks.

So accordingly, I had divided my time with extra efforts on Essay and Optional, in GS I had tried collecting value addition material to give the extra edge (explained below). In the end I was handsomely rewarded in the Optional paper (jump by 66 marks), while all GS papers combined, in absolute terms, marks (452) were less than last year (458) but relatively, I am sure, it would I have been in top 5-10 in the country.

However, essay (100) was somehow again on the lower side but as per me, my performance was best and I let the mystery remain unsolved if I that also try to find the answer that why I had scored low. These was as increase by 6 marks in the interview. So overall, I would say that expect the eassy paper, all the areas where I worked showed a lot of improvement that helped me achieve a good rank.

So, once again, I would advise all aspirants to introspect their weaknesses and rectify them. Persistence and dedicated hardwork, would definitely help in sailing their ship through the turbulent waters of UPSC.

MESSAGE FOR THE NEWCOMERS

To be very honest I have never attended any motivational seminar for Civil Service exam as I never felt demotivated while preparing for this exam despite challenges arising.

As per psychology, motivation is repeated goal directed behavior so I would say that always I had clear long and short term goals which were moderately challenging, but achievable hence I always strived to achieve them.

Unlike the vicious cycle of getting poor results and getting more demotivated I was lucky enough to be in a virtuous cycle of achieving my goals and getting more motivated. This led to improvements with each passing day which developed a belief that I was getting nearer to my ultimate goal, this kept the motivation high. I would partially credit this to a well thought and conscious decision of entering into the civil services. I had left a well paying job to prepare for an exam as unpredictable as UPSC, however as it was my own conscious choice so I never felt burdened in the preparation phase despite following the same routine for about 28 months. So only when you have an internal motivation and a burning desire to succeed then only you can sustain this journey.

WHAT WAS YOUR BOOK LIST?

I have a very concise book list. Most of the other toppers say, "Nothing was separate for Mains and Prelims as broadly the syllabus overlaps". I say that I have studied the following books religiously.

GS-1

Modern History: Spectrum alone, nothing else

Ancient and Medieval: Old NCERT's only + Vajiram Class Notes (Jain Sir)

World History: Vision IAS material + IAS4Sure notes (few topics)

Art N culture: Nitin Singhania Notes (not book) + Vajiram Jain Sir class notes

Geography: Mrunal videos + NCERT 11 th class only (both) + ATLAS

Society: Nothing specific + Vajiram class notes, nothing deep here just a broad understanding of key terminologies in syllabus.

GS-2

Polity (Static): Lakshmikanth

Polity (Current): VISION IAS monthly + Hindu

IR: Vision IAS monthly + Hindu

Governance: SRIRAM IAS class notes + 2nd ARC summary (selected portions)

GS-3

Econmics (Static): Sriram IAS material + Vajiram class notes

Economics (Current): VISION IAS monthly + Hindu + Economic Survey

Environment: Shankar IAS + VISION IAS monthly + Hindu

Security issues: Understanding key definitions +VISION IAS monthly + Hindu + selected portions from 2nd ARC summary.

Science Tech: Nothing specific being a science student + VISION IAS monthly + Hindu + Basic Biotechnology/Space/Disease related topics

Disaster management: 2nd ARC summary chapter + VISION IAS monthly + Hindu

Gs-4

(Psycho and Pub Ad related concepts)- Vajiram Class notes

Mrunal.org: Ethics notes and videos (explained in very lucid manner)

General understanding of all the keywords in the syllabus

PLANNING OF THE PREPARATION AS A BEGINNER

For this, I will advice to watch the video link (Mrunal.org). Following is a broad timeline for the same. I assumed starting of preparation 1 year before Prelims but one may tweak the same as per his/her circumstances, resources and situations.

Initial 7-8 months

- Read 1 subject/ month on your own for General Studies.
- Write at least 2 answers for Mains daily and 1 essay each 15 days.
- Finish classes / self preparation or whatever required for a good base in the optional subject.
- Get a fairly decent command over different areas of the syllabus

Next 1-2 months

Solve few Prelims papers' and start making notes for areas in GS in a manner that you are able to revise them later (includes static areas as well).

Do not make them bulky so that they become a separate book altogether nor so concise that they are unable to cover major portions.

Solving few Prelims' papers and having written few mains' answers will give you a fair enough idea of what to include in notes and what to exclude.

Last 2 months before Prelims

Focus on solving prelims tests, revision of notes that you have made, strategizing for the final prelims.

Next 40 days after prelims, before results are out

Be most cautious, do not waste these 40 days in speculation. Complete at least one reading / notes of optional. After this I believe that each of the sincere aspirant may not require any more spoon feeding in terms of planning the preparation. Join a test series for optional and GS and start giving their test. DO NOT fall in the trap of completing the full syllabus before attempting the tests (in GS).

ROLE OF COACHING INSTITUTES IN PREPARATION

I am no big fan of coaching when it comes to general studies provided one has had a decent school education. Only few areas like Polity, Economics may require some guidance. However honestly, as a beginner I was also insecure and had limited online resources, so I had joined Vajiram's classroom program. There also apart from Polity, Economics and few other classes I avoided all other classes where I thought extensive spoon feeding was going on (they literally dictate notes as if we are school students).

So my final opinion is that if one has absolutely no guidance then one can join separate classes for areas like Polity, Economics, may be Ethics just to build a solid base. History, Geography, Society, Science Tech etc can be easily managed by self study. Some people fully rely upon the coachings to finish the syllabus, but is turns out to be a big blunder and it should be avoided. Irrespective of whatever is going in a class we should always try to study the same ourselves independently. This will help in two ways, to revision and better understanding.

To give an analogy about the usefulness of the coachings, let us understand it by the construction of any building. Any building has a bare skeleton which is then furnished and given final finishing and it becomes pleasant for the eyes. Similarly coachings can be useful to lay that bare skeleton. Once skeleton is up then it depends on each individual candidate how he gives his final finishing over the skeleton.

❑❑

6

Name: Garima Agrawal
Rank: 40-CSE 2018, 241-CSE 2017

"Genius is 1% talent and 99% percent hard work." – Einstein

GARIMA AGRAWAL

OPTIONAL SUBJECT
Philosophy

MEDIUM
English

NATIVE PLACE
Khargone

EDUCATIONAL QUALIFICATION
- Btech and MS in ECE from IIIT-Hyderabad

PARENTS' OCCUPATION
- **Father:** Businessman
- **Mother:** Housewife

COACHING TAKEN
- Vajiram and Ravi, Delhi

MARKS
Prelims: Paper -1: 106 and Paper -2: 147.5

MAINS MARKS AND PERSONALITY TEST
GS: 438
Optional: 274
Interview: 193

MY JOURNEY

(a) Struggle during preparation and lessons learnt

When we start our preparations, we all start with a lot of fears, apprehensions and doubts regarding our background, our abilities and our competition. But my experiences and result have given some befitting answers to those doubts. Here are a few dominant ones-

❖ Yes, I have done my entire schooling from Khargone – a remote town of Madhya Pradesh. And still, I could clear the exam in one and half year of preparation.

(b) A remote background is not a hindrance to your success

❖ Yes, I have done my schooling in HINDI MEDIUM, but still I wrote all my exams including IIT-JEE and UPSC in English . It is a bit challenging but language is not a barrier but just a medium of expression.

❖ Yes, I am an engineer from IIIT-H and it was a tough decision to take up Civil Services instead of lucrative job/PhD offers. But having belief in the decision taken, helps you surpass any insecurity.

❖ Yes, I am a woman and still have put IPS as one of my preference because I genuinely feel that more representation of women in police will go a long way in women's security.

Last but not the least, if I can do it, anybody can.

Booklist

Polity: LaxmiKanth

History: Spectrum and modern India NCERT

Environment: Shankar IAS

Economics: K Shankar Ganesh

Geography: 11th and 12th NCERT

IR, SCI Tech: Current booklets

(c) **Preparation Strategy**

PRELIMS & MAINS

While everyone is well aware of the essential booklist for the exam, I would like to share some other strategies and tips that may help.

- Integrated study plan for Prelims and Mains for General Studies. Have a detailed timetable (monthly, weekly and daily) to read and revise all standard books keeping requirements of both Prelims and Mains in mind while studying.

  For example, if you are doing a topic of polity- Ordinance from M. Laxmikant, you should read the constitutional provisions for prelims but also read about the Cooper case and D.C. Wadhwa case (which is mentioned on the same page) for Mains. And then, linking it further to the current affairs completes your topic.

- Revision via tests. Sectional tests make the revision process interesting and fun while preparing you for the final exam at the UPSC. It is all the more important for Mains where answer writing and time management is indispensable for success.

- Innovative techniques for current affairs. Using sticky notes in front of your study table to remember tricky facts, watching daily videos of current affairs MCQ and of course reading newspaper with operatic regularity helps in handling current affairso. Writing two answers daily, based on current affairs really helps in preparing for GS2, 3, 4. Ram aple

- Study SMART. Studying smart means studying with mental alertness and as per the requirement of the exam. To illustrate- if you have to prepare Indian Ocean Rim Association (IORA) for prelims, a smart candidate would NOT memorize names of all 21 member states, but rather will look at the map and memorize only those states which are located on Indian Ocean but are NOT a member of IORA (Pakistan and Myanmar in this case). This makes the job much easier and helps you solve any question associated.

- Previous years' question papers are the MOST important guides for each stage of the examination- Prelims-GS, CSAT and Mains including Optional.

- Essay and Optional papers are pivotal in qualifying Mains and final selection. Consolidated notes for Optional subject and practice tests aid you in maximizing your score.

PERSONALITY TEST

My score in PT (190) is the silver lining in my marks sheet. The preparation involved, reading two newspapers, watching RSTV shows, systematic preparation of DAF (Detailed Application Form) and many mock interviews.

However, what helped me the most in my final interview was – (a) presence of mind and (b) the personality that I had developed over the years.

❑❑❑

7

Name: Vikram Grewal
Rank: 51, CSE-2018

"If you can dream—and not make dreams your master; If you can think—and not make thoughts your aim; If you can meet with Triumph and Disaster And treat those two impostors just the same...... Yours is the earth and everything that's in it..."

VIKRAM GREWAL

OPTIONAL SUBJECT
History

MEDIUM
English

NATIVE PLACE
Kurukshetra

EDUCATIONAL QUALIFICATION
❖ BA (History Hons)

PARENTS' OCCUPATION
❖ **Father:** Army Officer, ❖ **Mother:** Homemaker

COACHING TAKEN
❖ GS – Not taken. But regular Online Test Series from various sites like vision, Rau's, insights.

MARKS
Prelims: Paper -1: 126 and **Paper -2:** 155

MAINS MARKS AND PERSONALITY TEST
Essay (Paper I): 161
General Studies- I (Paper II): 86
General Studies- II (Paper III): 106
General Studies- III (Paper IV): 106
General Studies- IV (Paper V): 111
Optional - (History) (Paper I): 133
Optional - (History) (Paper II): 142
Interview: 190 ❖ Final Total: 1035

CONTACT
Twitter @vgrewal0

MOTIVATION MESSAGE AND STRATEGY

In times of distress I search for refuge in poetry.

The preparation for UPSC Civil Services Exam 2018 was a journey that needed a song that I could hum along the way. A journey that needed pointers spread across my way to assure myself that I was on the right path. It was a period in my life that needed words of inspiration on a daily basis.

And I found strength in the words of Kipling:

"If you can wait and not be tired by waiting,

Or being lied about, don't deal in lies,

Or being hated, don't give way to hating,

And yet don't look too good, nor talk too wise:"

Through this verse, I realized that it held the essence of the Civil Services examination as a whole. It is a struggle of the mind with itself. A test of character. A mission that demands persistence, consistency and optimism. It does look for knowledge in the candidate but more than that it searches for the 'application' of that knowledge.

Above all, UPSC probes a youthful mind to seek 'equilibrium' in it. 'BALANCE' is the foremost quality that the examination attempts to bring out in an aspirant. A balanced mind with an adaptable viewpoint- an empathetic perspective that would be able to understand the problems of the nation. An understanding that would accommodate the views of people from different strata of the society. A mind that has clarity of thought and yet is aware of its ignorance. That is what a generalist attitude implies. All inclusive and forward looking.

With balance, comes ORIGINALITY OF EXPRESSION. A mind that embraces the positives and negatives of an issue is able to put forward innovative solutions. UPSC considers that in high regard, especially in Mains and Personality Test stages. Even in Prelims, a balanced opinion gives way to understanding questions comprehensively which reduces the chances of marking a wrong option.

When it comes to strategizing about the exam, candidates tend to forget all the above characteristics and give way to a web of complexities. This brings me to another chief attribute that UPSC looks for and that is SIMPLICITY! Strategies to succeed should be plain and simple:

- ❖ Consult the syllabus regularly.
- ❖ Read the basic books esp. NCERTs; don't have multiple sources.
- ❖ Collect data from newspapers, Daily- Monthly- Annual compilations.
- ❖ Make precise notes and revise them.
- ❖ Practice Mock Tests under exam conditions (I gave Insights IAS prelims test series-2018.)
- ❖ (Each successive step is more important than its preceding one.)

During the journey, your Simplicity will be challenged in the form of coaching institute's extra classes, seniors' advice, relatives' suggestions and your WhatsApp/Telegram groups. The key is to not lose track of your SIMPLE strategy.

Do not increase your materialistic capacities with more books, notes and teachers; increase your thinking capacity! It is a mental battleground that ticks by the watch and jousts by the pen. Knowledge is power, yes! But you need to be selective about its usage. You can only carry limited number of arrows in your quiver. The point is to OPTIMALLY use them.

Too much knowledge makes your baggage heavy and slows you down; but a swift brain can increase your speed. Hence, use mnemonics, abbreviations and self-made tricks to enhance your memory which will improve your chances of identifying the right option in prelims. Moreover, CRITICAL THINKING is crucial. By making a SWOT analysis of issues you can make better notes and score well in answer writing.

Next up, being REGULAR and DISCIPLINED is indispensable. No matter what your strategy is, it is pointless if you are not consistent with it. To stay regular, have a do-able prep routine. Divide your day into small sessions and fill in the breaks with constructive rejuvenation activities. For example, listening to All India Radio, watching a documentary film, meditating and your favourite playlist can work wonders for your concentration and prepare your GS, Ethics, Essay papers simultaneously.

That being said, don't be a TECH-SLAVE. Use internet wisely. Restrain from social media and save time! TIME IS THE ULTIMATE BOSS! "You mess with it, it'll mess you up."

Finally and most importantly, you need a SOLID SUPPORT SYSTEM. This can be your parents, friends, relatives or anyone who understands your aims and aspirations, who can keep the fire in your belly burning. Find in the daily monotony, springs of inspiration. It can be Rafi's voice or Kate McKinnon's comedy or Sahir's lyrics or Keith Richards' riffs or anything under the sun.

Awaken the curious child inside you. All the answers are half-asleep inside you. Reading and writing will only help you stir it up. And that's the underlying message of this exam. The journey to become a good civil servant begins with being a good student for (and of) life and its manifestations which include success and failure.

❑❑

8

Name: Sumit Kumar Rai
Rank: 54, CSE-2018

'UPSC journey is full of unpredictability. There will be moments of failures at various stages. What is important is protecting yourself in all such moments.'

SUMIT KUMAR RAI

OPTIONAL SUBJECT
Public Administration

MEDIUM
English

NATIVE PLACE
Gopalganj, Bihar

EDUCATIONAL QUALIFICATION
❖ Dual Degree (B.Tech+ M.Tech) in Petroleum Engineering from IIT (ISM) Dhanbad (2008-2013)

PARENTS' OCCUPATION
❖ **Father:** Agriculture
❖ **Mother:** Homemaker

COACHING TAKEN
❖ GS – None
❖ Optional – None
❖ Answer writing Practice- Forum IAS (for GS & Essay), Vision IAS (for essay), Lukmaan (for ethics)

MARKS
Prelims: Paper -1: 106 and **Paper -2:** 120

MAINS MARKS AND PERSONALITY TEST
Essay (Paper I): 127
General Studies- I (Paper II): 098
General Studies- II (Paper III): 098
General Studies- III (Paper IV): 119
General Studies- IV (Paper V): 104
Optional - (Pub. Ad.) (Paper I): 150
Optional - (Pub. Ad.) (Paper II): 157
Total: 853
Interview: 182
Final Total: 1035

CONTACT OPTIONS

Facebook:https://www.facebook.com/sumitrai007

Instagram:https://www.instagram.com/sumitkumarrai_ias/

Twitter:https://https://twitter.com/skrias2018

Blog:https://sumitkumarrai.com

Quora: https://www.quora.com/profile/Sumit-Kumar-Rai

MY JOURNEY

'Nahi hua' I said these words to my mother on the evening of 27th April 2018 with a sad face and a sunk heart. I could even see the deeper sadness in her eyes. It was my 4th attempt, 2nd interview and I was not in the list, again. I have seen failures earlier also, thanks to the journey that UPSC is, but the pain that my mother was unable to conceal was more heart wrenching than anything. I decided two things on that day: I have to get over this anyhow (Rage, rage against the dying of the light. ...Yeah, that's what I said to myself when the light within me was dying) and I should not be at home when next CSE results would be declared.

Treading with a job: travails of a working aspirant

I joined Cairn India as a petroleum engineer in 2013 and have given all my 5 attempts with a job. Managing preparation along with job is a tedious task and needs lots of planning, perseverance, passion and a strong-will.

❖ First of all, you need to have a mindset about your current job. It should be treated as a temporary phenomenon in your life. Assume that it is just a job, it is not something where you want to spend your entire life. Your passion and that burning desire for civil services should be your guiding criteria at your work place. So, treat your job as it is: it is secondary to your preparation. By this I don't mean that you became too negligent at work. That should not be the case and an aspiring civil servant should never do that. You should have that adequate level of efficiency and professionalism and you should be able to complete all your deliverables within time. But you should avoid all those other things which can be otherwise utilized for your preparation (Social gatherings, frequent parties, Office gossip, extended lunch hours etc.). Don't run after appraisals. Even if you get a bad one, it is not the end of your life. A little sacrifice is needed for a noble cause.

- I did not let anyone know in the office that I was preparing. I prepared in silence, so that success can roar. As there are practical problems especially in the private sector, so I decided to keep this as my little secret.
- I decided to plan my time judiciously which I would get after the office hours. I divided my time between optional and GS and studied accordingly. Also, I never expected to run at super efficiency speed every time. On many days I never felt like reading but it's ok to feel so. What is not ok is making it a too recurrent phenomenon at that point of time, I used to remind myself. "No, that's not how my story is going to end. Fall you must, but fail you shouldn't. And I used to come out of the comfort zone and start reading.
- I felt weekends as God's gift to me and used them to the fullest.
- Social media: Since I had time constraints, I stayed stay away from social media as much as possible. Instead, read newspapers and do productive things. I was away from Facebook for a long time, didn't use WhatsApp much and got active only after this year's result. So everything can wait: Said this to myself always.
- I made my mobile as my best friend, and it is more so for working-travelling aspirants. You can read on flights, in trains, in office washrooms if you have that one companion. So I made my mobile my library.
- 'Remember why you started in the first place': Remember this line in case you want to quit,there was a bad day at office, you felt like a failure or when you were just too helpless in this lone, long journey at any point of time.
- I avoided conflicts at my workplace as much as possible. They would have my hampered preparation I kept my eyes on UPSC.

In the end, I would like to leave you with my personal journey:

I failed in prelims 2014, I failed in mains 2015, and I reached till interview stage in next two attempts (2016 & 2017). In 4 attempts, I had seen my heart shattered many times and each time it was damn difficult to start again. Many said that you had such a high paying job and you should not be worrying about UPSC this much. But how could I do that? How could I give up? The heart doesn't lie.

So I kept going.

I was very clear that I will try till my very last and even if I fail at the end of my 6th attempt, I would be happy with the feeling that I failed rather than I never tried.

I never wanted to have that regret: What if?

Message for new comers:

Will it be difficult? **Yes**

Will it be impossible? **No**

The UPSC journey is full of unpredictability. There will be moments of failures at various stages. What is important is protecting yourself in all such moments. I say this because I know how difficult it is to not see your name in the pdf, either after pre, after mains or after interview.

In those dark moments be a little kinder to yourself. Look in the mirror, look at the person looking in the mirror, feel a little proud of the journey you have taken so far, sacrifices made so far. Give that person a pat on the back, and smile a little bit. 'Not today' as Syrio Forel told Arya Stark, you tell yourself the same thing… 'Not today'. Today is not the day you let your guards down. Be the finest warrior you are. Be the best on those days. It's a game of mental strength. You need to become that person, same way Arya stark becomes the sharpest warrior through years of pain and training.

You should be able to access Laxmikanth pdf within 30 seconds, read your optional notes and should be able to make online notes on ever note (or any other platform). So, a good investment in mobile with lots of storage space is recommended.

- Choose your friends selectively. Avoid noisy ones. Be in company of people who motivate you and create positivity in your life. Have someone who has absolute faith in you all the time, they do wonders for you.
- Form a close group of friends and discuss questions, your answer sheets and learn cumulatively.
- Be respectful and kind, everyone you meet is fighting a different battle. So be a little kinder, it is what makes you humane. Help someone at work, it will make you feel good. It helps in civil services preparation somehow—blessings and positive energy.
- Never give up, avoid taking decisions in a haste especially after a setback like a failure in prelims, mains or finally not getting selected in the end. Give yourself a week's time and get back in the preparation mode again.

  Success will be there eventually with such an attitude.

❑❑

9

Name: Manisha Rana
Rank: 67, CSE-2018

"The difference between ORDINARY and EXTRAORDINARY is that LITTLE EXTRA."

MANISHA RANA

OPTIONAL SUBJECT
Mathematics

MEDIUM
English

NATIVE PLACE
Kheda Kalan; New Delhi

EDUCATIONAL QUALIFICATION
- B.Tech – BITS PILANI

PARENTS' OCCUPATION
- **Father:** Retired Army Officer
- **Mother:** Homemaker

COACHING TAKEN
- GS – Sriram
- Mathematics – IMS

MAINS MARKS AND PERSONALITY TEST

Essay (Paper I): 130
General Studies- I (Paper II): 105
General Studies- II (Paper III): 099
General Studies- III (Paper IV): 112
General Studies- IV (Paper V): 100
Optional - (Mathematics) (Paper I): 155
Optional - (Mathematics) (Paper II): 171
Total: 872
Interview: 157
Final Total: 1029

MY JOURNEY

How to overcome the ups/down?

- It was my 4th attempt this time. I in my previous 3 attempts, I couldn't clear the exam after interview, not even once. So ups and downs are a part of the process, one should never lose hope and have faith that hard work will payoff ultimately. Sometimes you will have people who will underestimate you, sometimes you yourself will underestimate your own potential. But this is exactly what makes this journey interesting. It teaches you a lot of life lessons of patience, perseverance, determination, hard work, luck and interplay of all these.
- Civil services exam is an area where hard work and luck both play a very important role which makes it unpredictable and so one should always have alternative career options in mind for mental peace and a fall back.
- To keep your motivation level high, you can listen to motivational music, you can read motivational quotes, read about the journey of other successful candidates and gather your inspiration from them and also attempting test papers of Prelims and Mains will help you keep your energy level high. Also, strategy in the exam is way more important than hard work.
- I would highly recommend watching videos of vision IAS, those on telegram groups, Mrunal and also reading the articles of toppers given by insights and other Websites which help you get a sense of direction as well as motivation to keep working hard. At the same time one should not ignore one's physical health and should regularly exercise to decrease the level of stress.
- Rest, after working in Indian Forest Service for two years I can say that life is much beyond an exam. Do whatever it takes, but don't let your happiness be dependent on success in the exam. Keep a positive outlook, be a good human being, work hard and never ever lose hope.

  Nothing matters but your true will, to succeed in life....

❑❑

10

Name: Dilip Pratap Singh Shekhawat
Rank: 72, CSE-2018

A JOURNEY FROM GULLY BOY TO IAS

DILIP PRATAP SINGH SHEKHAWAT

OPTIONAL SUBJECT
Public Administration

MEDIUM
English

NATIVE PLACE
Jodhpur

EDUCATIONAL QUALIFICATION
- B. Tech in Chemical Engineering

PARENTS' OCCUPATION
- **Father:** Manager in a Private firm
- **Mother:** Homemaker

MARKS

Prelims: Paper -1: 98.66 and Paper -2: 140.00

MAINS MARKS AND PERSONALITY TEST
Essay (Paper I): 150
General Studies- I (Paper II): 080
General Studies- II (Paper III): 118
General Studies- III (Paper IV): 095
General Studies- IV (Paper V): 092
Optional - (Pub.Ad.) (Paper I): 160
Optional - (Pub.Ad.) (Paper II): 154
Written Total: 849
Personality Test: 179
Final Total: 1028

MY JOURNEY

(a) A flashback into my childhood

When elders used to ask me the clichéd question – Beta, 'Bade hokar kya banna chahte ho?', unlike other children of Middle class society, who used to reply Doctor, Teacher, engineer, etc., I used to say that 'Mai Cricketer banna chahta hu'. Such a statement from me always resulted in laughter or criticism. People around me always made fun out of such a response from my side. The most common reply was 'Har koi Sachin nahi ban sakta'. But, still my motivation was strong enough to ignore such responses.

Initially, in my school days, I was completely dedicated and devoted to cricket. On one evening my coach said 'Give me 2 years, I will get you selected in Indian cricket team'. Such a statement from my coach was very inspiring for me. I committed myself to it. But, then the family drama started. That time I was in 12th Class, a very crucial juncture of my life which had to shape my career. My father, a like any other typical middle class father was strictly against my pursuit of cricket as a career. Ultimately after some resistance, I succumbed to the pressure and gave up cricket and started to focus on studies.

(b) My tryst with academics

In my entire schooling career, I was a below average student, who was only concerned about passing the class- by how much, didn't matter. After my breakup with cricket, I was thrown into a very hostile world of competitive exams, viz. IIT-JEE, AIEEE, etc. But, when a person is under severe pain, he struggles, he strives, he makes an effort, and that effort landed me in National Institute of Technology, Rourkela after clearing the AIEEE exam with All India Rank 14821.

Now, 14821 may not sound to be a very good rank, but the purpose was served, that is freedom from parenting, gully friends, the society, the city and also myself, who had once failed in life by giving up cricket.

(c) The wrong choice

In the final round of counseling for engineering colleges, I was hoping to get MNIT Jaipur or SVNIT Surat. Hopes failed me once again and I was allotted Chemical Engineering at NIT Rourkela. When I first saw the results of the last round of College allocation, I was in utter shock and despair as NIT Rourkela was completely unexpected as per the previous year trends and ranking. NIT Rourkela pulled me from a completely different culture of the west to a very different culture of Eastern India. For a person who has spent his entire childhood and schooling in one town this was a challenging path ahead.

Still, I summoned up the courage and started alone to seek admission in NIT Rourkela. After reaching Rourkela, I encountered a completely alien world with different culture, food, people, vegetation, etc. I straightaway slipped into depression and even made up my mind to leave the College and go home. At that time, when I was about to resign, a gentleman in the College Academic office advised me to reconsider my decision and stay back. I looked into the past and recalled my give up moment in life, that is leaving Cricket as a career, Then, I realized that giving up on Cricket didn't make me happy and left me with lifelong regret. I made a firm commitment to never give up in life. From here the journey from a Gully boy to IAS began.

(d) The motivation to prepare for civil services

I never in my wildest dreams thought of becoming an IAS officer. I never had any Idea about either IAS or Civil Services. And when I got some Idea about Civil Services, I also came to know that this exam is also reputed as the toughest exam in the world, hence, no chance for a below average student like me. But, I am fond of Bollywood movies. A dialogue in the movie "Om Shanti OM" goes like – "Agar kisi cheez ko poori shiddat se chaho, to saari kaynaat tumhe apni manzil se milane me jut jaati hai".

Life me ek kaam badi shiddat se kiya- Social Service through the platform of Lions Club, NIT Rourkela. I joined the Club in the first year of my college. We used to get involved in Social Service activities like Teaching underprivileged children, serving old age homes and orphanages, organizing blood donation camps, etc. Though we did all these activities on a very small scale but always felt a sense of happiness and satisfaction by serving the people, understanding their problems and attempting to resolve their issues. This intrinsic sense of happiness and satisfaction became a true motivation for me to attempt for the Civil Services, Still, in the 4 years of my College, I never thought about attempting Civil Services. I was even placed in a private firm in the Campus placements in my Final year and was finally prepared to join the job.

(e) The tumultuous dilemma

After leaving the college in May 2015, I went home and was waiting for the joining in the company in which I was placed. But as the time was passing, the joining letter was also not coming. On a fine day in June, the result of the

CDS 2015 Written exam came and I qualified for the SSB. At this point, I considered UPSC Civil Services as a career option. Some of my seniors were already preparing for UPSC and they also ignited my interest in Civil Services. Hence, I came across a big dilemma,that is whether to go for a secure job or to venture into the wilderness of Civil Services. My mind was inclined towards going for the private job but my heart was inclined in preparing for the Civil Services.

At this juncture again, I recalled my childhood days when I gave up on cricket in lieu of uncertainty and fierce competition in the game. But, then I connected the dots that If I work really very hard with complete dedication and devotion, I might enter into the Civil Services as my heart lies in Civil Services. I conveyed to my parents that I have failed once in life and the regret of becoming a cricketer always haunts me. I have got this second chance in life to pursue a career where my heart lies, please let me take the risk. In this way I convinced my parents to let me take the risk and prepare for the Civil services. Hence, I got the NOC from the Home Ministry and went ahead to pursue Civil Services preparation in Delhi.

(f) A ray of hope in the ocean of uncertainty

When I came to Delhi in July 2015 I was hit with heavy depression. When I entered into the Main Road of Old Rajinder Nagar, I saw thousands of UPSC aspirants jam-packed on the one way towards IAS. I, coming from a humble background with no great academic achievement found myself lost in this vast ocean of uncertainty. Hit with such a trauma, I even thought of going back home and do something matching my average calibre. At this moment, I again referred to my conscience, and the answer was give your best, and leave the rest.

After initially staying at my friend's home, I started hunting for a room in Old Rajinder Nagar. After hunting a dozen of the rooms in ORN, me and my friend settled for a 1+1 Room flat near PUSA road. For food, we joined a tiffin service serving some delicious food – "Swaad aisa ki Ghar ki yaad aa jaye". The tiffin did realize its Tag line. Such me har din 2 time ghar ki aur maa ki yaad aa jati thi, after eating a more water than grain dal and a more maida than wheat roti. In ORN, everything was monetized and commercialized. Humanity was like an endangered species, difficult to find in classrooms, mess, brokers, etc. But, still I thank my family and friends to be there for me in those difficult times. Hence, I stood strong and passed the initial phase of my preparation in Delhi.

(g) An encounter with sleepless nights

After the initial phase of preparation when there was a sudden and multiple bombardment of Class lectures, notes, books, test series, etc., my untrained below average mind was unable to process all this at once. Hence, such a phenomena resulted in huge and sustained shortage of sleep. I started to force myself to sleep without any success. My top search on Google was 'How to treat insomnia'. But, then a realized that there is no point lying awake in the bed and wasting time. I started to study till I automatically got sleepy.

This phase of my preparation was very important as during this time by beating anxiety and fear, I was able to complete most of my syllabus of GS and Optional in that time.

(h) The unforgivable mistake

In April 2016, as my coaching got over, I made a stupid decision to go home. I left ORN because of twin sets of reasons. One, I could not to bear the hostile environment of ORN and I was sure that my efficiency of studying would increase with good moral support of my mother. The first reason was still valid but the second reason backfired. Instead of moral support, I was feeling a good amount of moral pressure to clear the exam as early as possible.

But, despite a number of challenges at home (e.g.: doing household work, tolerating relatives' questions, etc.) I persisted and took my first attempt from Jodhpur. My CSE 2016 Preliminary exam on 7th August did go well, as I was having a feel good factor after the paper and after calculating the marks I was getting around 118 marks. The expected cut off predicted by a bunch of coaching institutes was around 110. Hence, this was a booster for me and to make it up for my earlier mistake I again went back to Delhi for joining Test series and doing my CSE 2016 Main examination preparation.

(i) The September horror

After moving to Delhi in September, I aggressively started preparing for the CSE 2016 Main examination. I worked day in and day out to give a good shot at the Main examination. But, all went in vain as I could not find my Roll no. in the list of qualified candidates for the Main exam, when the result was declared on the evening of 16th September, 2016. It was a moment of utter shock and sorrow for me as I had good expectations from the result. Suddenly, all the sunshine in my life went away and I was left with empty darkness. In an examination, in which I devoted one complete year of my life dumped me and I was left with no recourse at all.

But, after a few days of sorrow and gloom, I again had to decide for myself: whether to persist in UPSC or to exit and look for an easier option in life. But, when I looked back into the CSE 2016 Preliminary Exam, I could easily find that I was very close and also I could identify my mistakes. It was evident in the marksheet also: I got 115.34 marks and the official cut off was 116. I took the result positively and started the preparation again with a very strong resolve that I was not going to be in this situation again.

Henceforth, I started preparation for Mains 2017 in full swing by special focus on Current affairs notes, answer writing practice, writing test series, etc. Here, my vision was very clear that had I given Mains 2016, I may not have cleared it as I had little command over answer writing and Current affairs ; but, when I clear Prelims 2017, I must clear Mains 2017 with a very good margin.

(j) Physical Examination of CAPF 2017

Below is the blog post written by my younger brother during my preparation of Physical Examination of CAPF. It had been 1 year since starting the preparation, so it was an additional challenge to prepare for it. My brother talked to me at least once a week, so he had fair bit of idea about my preparation for both the challenges. Blog:

> *"This post is totally dedicated to my brother DJ, who has so many qualities, that it is difficult to put all in one place. Yet I will try to write those down.*
>
> *He is currently preparing for UPSC, and this is his second year running. It has been 2 years, he has left everything for accomplishing his dreams. Friends, enjoyment, sports are all alien to him now. If my dedication towards anything is x, then his dedication for UPSC is 10^ (6)x. He has chosen this way of life and I deeply respect his decision. Not everyone is brave enough to spend his youth in pursuit of greatness when that means to sacrifice each and everything. He didn't go to convocation, to take his degree, which for many is a lifetime opportunity to look back to those days of enjoyment. I don't know how he manages to sacrifice so much, just for the sake of his objective in life. I know it is a big deal, but truly how many of us say no to those little enjoyment, which we readily believe we 'should get' for 'the effort we are putting!' Not much, I know for sure.*
>
> *Up till now, he has given 3 papers. UPSC Prelims 2016, RAS Prelims 2016, and CRPF 2016.*

He couldn't get through UPSC prelims. He got around 118, which was a big yes for qualification for Mains by many coaching institutes in Delhi. This came as a shock for him as he was already preparing for Mains last year. He couldn't clear RAS Pre due to valid reasons (I will discuss those later). He qualified CRPF prelims, appear for Mains, qualified that also. He gave his medical in which he was marked 'overweight' with one more attempt at reducing weight in about 1 month's time. He was 90 Kgs that time and the limit was 78 Kgs. He sought advice for nearby Gyms in Delhi, and everywhere he was given the same inference that it was not possible to reduce 12 Kgs in a month; maximum they could reduce was 7 Kgs. He took it as a challenge.

He followed a strict diet pattern. Breakfast: Almonds, Lemon, Honey. Lunch: An apple. Dinner: Oats (boiled). He carried that this for a month. I know it is incorrect to skip the efforts that he put day in and day out. Eating the same things everyday, same oats everyday. Ignoring the hunger. I believe hunger can make people do things like revolutions. But here is a man who forgets what he likes to eat just to qualify for an Interview of Class B CRPF officer. I cannot control my hunger for even 2 days. If I skipped a meal, my next breakfast would be heavy as hell. He lost around 15 Kgs. He weighed was around 75 Kgs.

The date for re-medical was getting postponed and he kept reducing his diet everyday. Near the medical dates he constricted the diet more and more, to a level that just before 2-3 days, he hardly ate anything. 'Just to be sure'. He was feeling very weak at those times and could hardly study. During the re-medical, he recalled that he felt immense weakness and could have fallen on the ground. His weight was 69 Kgs, far lower that the expected cutoff. I think his resolve for reducing the weight is massive achievement in itself. How many of us can achieve this feat? Honestly, I cannot.

He gave 2 mock interviews, which were his first ones of their kind. He gave his final interview on 16th Jan, 2017.

On 8th of Feb, 2017, the much awaited result of CRPF came. He hadn't qualified. I had my GATE-2017 paper on 12th Feb. He waited for 12th and after coming back to the room, he shared some light moments. My paper had gone well and I felt a sigh of relief. We talked for an hour or so, after which he broke the news. He was sad, from the inside, and I could sense it on his face. So much sacrifice he put in. This time 189, students were only recommended, much lesser than normally around 400. He made more drastic resolves to point where he had stopped going outside and has committed to giving much time to each paper starting from 1 March. This is in regard to the USCE Prelims-2017 being conducted in June.

I respect his decisions and stand by him on every front of his life. Because I know he can do things I cannot, even in my dreams. DJ, take a salute."

(k) The 2017 attempt: a big learning curve

In this attempt, I started early preparation for Prelims 2017, so that there was no doubt about writing Mains 2017. I solved around 70 Mock tests, made current affairs notes and did multiple revisions, revised the syllabus again and again.

My preliminary exam went well and I was expecting a sure call for Mains 2017. But, again thanks to my foolishness, I didn't join the test series for Mains 2017 just after Prelims 2017 was over. I waited stupidly for the results to be declared, so that I was sure of writing Mains 2017. In my subconscious mind, the horror of September 2016 was still there to haunt me. Ever after getting very safe marks I could not start preparing full fledged for Mains 2017, as in 2016 also I did the same and when the result was negative, all preparation for Mains went in vain. Hence, in this case Human Psychology trumped rationality.

Nevertheless, on 27th July 2017, the Prelims 2017 results were announced. Around 13000 candidates qualified for Mains 2017. I was ecstatic that I was one among those have the golden opportunity to write the Main exam. Though, I wasted a lot of time waiting for the result but started preparing for Mains 2017 with full vigour. I joined test series for Essay, GS and Optional and started to buck up and give my tests on a regular basis on par with other candidates. When the Mains 2017 exam arrived, I was very confident of clearing it.

I gave the Mains 2017 exam with full heart and was expecting an interview call. On 10th January, 2018, I indeed got an interview call. After, seeing my Roll no. in the Mains result, I was very relieved that my hardwork paid off and now I am only one step away from glory. At that time I was at home, and without wasting time I left for Delhi to prepare for the Interview.

(l) The horror of CSE 2017 interview

After preparing for around 2 months, I had my Interview on 23rd March, 2018 in the morning session. I called my mother to stay with me in Delhi during the interview, so that I am more calm and composed. The night before the

Interview, I was so nervous that I was unable to sleep due to anxiety and fear of failure. My interview was held in Dr. PK Joshi sir's board at UPSC Bhawan. My interview started on a very rough patch and I was asked some tough questions related to my Graduation (Chemical Engineering) and hobbies. I got nervous in the starting itself and was never able to get my confidence back. I got only 138 marks out of 275 in the interview, which ensured my rejection in the Final list of CSE 2017 by only 15 Marks. Though it was a very close miss, there was no consolatory prize for my hardwork and perseverance.

After the Interview, I had little hope of getting IAS selection. I left Delhi and went to Jodhpur again. This time to never come back to Delhi. The roadmap was vey clear. If I made to the list, I would improve my service to IAS and if not, I will prepare for RAS 2018 Exam for which I had applied after the Interview.

(m) 27th April 2018: A breaking point

On the evening of 27th April, 2018, the final result of CSE 2017 came. I was studying in my room when I saw the disturbance on social media about CSE 2017 results. Unfortunately, again I failed in this exam. This time I was completely broken after the declaration of result and I saw my mother who is a very strong person also breaking apart. This was a very tough time for me and my family. After 3 years of struggle I was again back to the starting point.

There was only 1 month left for CSE 2018 Prelims exam. The time with me was very less and insufficient to prepare for Prelims 2018 and too little after taking in consideration the recovery after such a huge setback in life. At that moment, I talked to one of my seniors in IAS and he suggested me to postpone the recovery part and fully focus on Prelims 2018.

(n) The Battle Axe of Prelims 2018

After the CSE 2018 final result there was only a month left for CSE 2018 Prelims. It was a situation like Battle of Haldighati between Akbar's forces (UPSC CSE 2017 failure plus Challenge of CSE 2018 Prelims) and Maharana Pratap (weakened by many failures in life plus huge damage by UPSC failure). But, I preferred to fight until my last breath and give my best in limited time. The day of Prelims exam was a very important day in my life. After decades, UPSC had set the toughest paper. It was like fighting a machine gun with a sword. But, I didn't care and gave the paper in full confidence –"Ya to aar ya paar "Attempted all 100 Questions in GS Paper 1 (an extremely foolish thing to do in Prelims exam due to Negative Marking). After calculating the Marks from various Answer keys I was scoring in the range of 98 to 104. I realized the GAME was OVER.

I shared my marks with my friends in Delhi and they exuded confidence in me and asked me to come to Delhi and start preparing for Mains 2018. Finally, I made a decision and came to Delhi for Mains 2018 preparation. But, after coming to Delhi, I was again involved in the wait for CSE Prelims 2018 result. I remember at that time, Football world cup was going on. Amidst anxiety and anticipation of Prelims 2018 result, I was not able to study for Mains 2018 and hence I watched all the Football matches and also roamed here and there with friends. Meanwhile, I got Viral fever in early July 2018 and around 10 days were completely wasted.

(o) The day of Prelims 2018 result

It was Saturday and I was just sitting in my library. My friend noticed some hulchul and gossip about result in his own library and he called me and asked my result. I also found out that the result has come. I swiftly left for my room as I didn't want to express my extreme emotions in library and feel embarrassed. When I checked the result in my Room, I screamed and jumped in the air. I had magically qualified for Mains 2018. Magically, because I had lost hope for a Positive result.

I immediately called my Mother and informed about her result. She was very happy that I qualified, otherwise, we as a family could even break apart. But, then I realized that this is the Final chance I have got and I made a strong commitment to myself – to never be in such a situation again.

(p) Mains 2018: Hard work + Smart work

After wasting around 45 days in anticipation and wait for result, I rigorously started preparing for Mains 2018. Hard work was involved in covering the syllabus and revising multiple times and smart work in focusing on Essay, GS Paper 2 and Public Administration, so that in such a less amount of time, I could prepare for more marks. This time the strategy worked and I cleared Mains 2018 by a good margin of around 80 marks.

(q) The final lap: CSE 2018 interview

The horror of CSE 2017 Interview was still fresh in my mind and hence for this attempt, I decided to start early for Interview preparation. I collaborated with my library friend and started discussing on various issues of National and International importance along with preparing the Bio-data (Detailed Application Form). This time, I had mentioned only one hobby- Heartfullness meditation under the guidance of Shri Ram Chandra Mission. I have immensely benefitted from Heartfullnes as it always gave me a right balance between materialism and spirituality, which helped me to find the right solution to difficult situations I found myself in.

After the Main examination result on 20th December, 2018, I started the Interview preparation full throttle. I formed whatsapp groups, collaborated with friends, gave Mock Interviews and hence left no stone unturned for best preparation of the Interview.

(r) Finally the day arrived

On 13th March, 2019 Afternoon, I had my UPSC CSE 2018 Interview. This time I was very calm, composed and relaxed. I also called upon my friends to have some fun in the morning and also accompany me to UPSC Bhavan. Before the actual interview, I was in a chilled mode and that did work in my favour in the interview as I was very confident throughout the whole interview. That day I learned that if you possess the qualities desirable in Civil Services like honesty, integrity, empathy, etc. then no one can stop you from getting selected but you yourself and your self doubt.

(s) The final result date

On 5th April, 2019, UPSC announced its final results for CSE 2019. That day from early morning there was gossip about result coming today. I became very anxious and called my friends to the room to relieve some stress sharing some light moments in such a heavy environment of result being round the corner. As the time passed, the anxiety was increasing. In the end, we decided to proceed to the UPSC Bhavan to physically check the result. When I reached there, there was result on the main notice board. It was

Hence, the Journey from a Gully boy to IAS was complete.

In the end, I can say that nothing matters but your true will, to succeed in life.

□□

11

Name: Pradeep Kumar Dwivedi
Rank: 74, CSE-2018

When your hopes, dreams and goals are in a same direction, then the way of achieving success gets easier.

PRADEEP KUMAR DWIVEDI

OPTIONAL SUBJECT
Hindi Literature

MEDIUM
English

NATIVE PLACE
Barigarh, Chatarpur

EDUCATIONAL QUALIFICATION
❖ B. Tech

PARENTS' OCCUPATION
❖ **Father:** Farmer
❖ **Mother:** House Wife

COACHING
Self Study

MAINS MARKS AND PERSONALITY TEST
Essay (Paper I): 116
General Studies- I (Paper II): 081
General Studies- II (Paper III): 102
General Studies- III (Paper IV): 114
General Studies- IV (Paper V): 106
Optional - (Hindi Litt.) (Paper I): 161
Optional - (Hindi Litt.) (Paper II): 183
Written Total: 863
Personality Test: 165
Final Total: 1028

MY JOURNEY

Friends, I am a native of the region of Bundelkhand, where the dream of getting the civil service is considered to be a difficult task.

The condition of road connectivity to Barigarh located at a distance of 75 kms from the district headquarters is that there is no bus facility from 6 o'clock in the evening to 9 o'clock in the morning from the nearest railway station Mahoba. If one does not have one's own vehicle, then people get stranded and are compelled to wait at the station for the whole night for the distance of only 15 kms. The last bus from the district headquarters leaves at 4 pm. Most of the educated youth are jobless and unemployed and migrating from one place to another for income is the main source of earning and employment.

In such a deplorable situation, a father envisioned a dream that he would give his son all that he himself had been unable achieve. That father had completed a diploma in electrical engineering, which was considered the toughest and great in those days, but due to the domestic responsibilities, he had to choose the farming as a source of earning. His father's wedding was organized at the early age of only 15 due to social customs and he became the father of 3 children at the age of 22 and he made them to dream this dream. This story, is of his elder son.

This boy was working hard with a calm and composed mind at the age of 7-8. He recalls with relief the better education provided by Navodaya Vidyalaya and the exemption of fees to be paid by his father.

This is the real story of Sri Pradeep Kumar Dwivedi , who secured 74th rank in this year's civil services examination. Pradeep Kumar's story who hails from Barigarh in Chhatarpur district may be a source of inspiration for many rural youth. If a person has determination, dedication and devotion towards his goal and objectives, surely at will be achieved one day.

When Pradeep got first position in the school in 10th standard, the journalist of Dainik Bhaskar asked him what you want to become - Pradeep's answer was to join the IAS. The journalist asked why- Pradeep replied that the bus coming from Chhatarpur to Barigarh with a distance of only 75 km is covered in 5 hours and many of the children are deprived of their real goal and dreams. I want to provide a smooth and easy access to everyone by bridging this distance.

Certainly, his the goal was to become an IAS officer, because Pradeep chose this as the only platform, where he could change something. Something that could make some people's lives better, but there is a difference between dreams and reality and it is not so easy to bridge these differences in the real world.

Pradeep was told that the easiest way to get a good job passes through the path of engineering and thus he hoping to reduce his father's financial burden and took admission in engineering. While studying in Manit, the idea of IAS crossed to Pradeep's mind but it did not come true. A PSU job was considered the best job for an engineer but he met with failure everywhere. Seeing nothing positive, Aditya finally got a private job in Virala. The job was good, but Pradeep was upset about not getting the government job, so he often used to appear in government's engineer examinations to be in government sector and he was selected for the post of Assistant Engineer at Electricity Department in Madhya Pradesh. In the beginning he was posted at sub-division Chichali located in Narsinghpur district and this posting again inspired him towards civil service. The condition of rural tribals and the pathetic condition of farmers was neither easy to improve with only power supply nor was it sufficient. At this time Pradeep felt that he was not on the platform where he could be and was not doing as much as his capabilities. Pradeep decided to materialize the dream of his civil service examination. The difficult posting at Jabalpur, made it impossible to focus on studies. So eventually he had to take a drastic decision to fulfil my dream. The decision was to leave the job. His family members and friends were not happy with the decision of leaving the job of a gazetted officer. Everyone had a genuine and legitimate doubt about success. But seeing Pradeep's confidence and faith, his father eventually accepted his decision. His father once again sacrificed his dreams and put the desire to build the house aside and the result is known to us, Pradeep secured 491th rank in 2017 and 74th in 2018.

Friends, Pradeep's story may be very simple and easy, but one thing is worth noting is that – to go to any extent to fulfill his dream, even if it is the decision of leaving the government job or to crack the civil exam with limited resources.

The other thing that appears in this story is high confidence and trust in oneself. Pradeep believes that there are only two types of work, one is what you want, what you always wanted to be and the other one that you had to be choose in compulsion seeing the circumstances. He thinks that if he has to make his career in any job then it could be done after attempting the civil services. He was confident that he would able to earn his livelihood and he gave this assurance to his father.

He is of the view that he does not want to live life with the pain of not trying for civil services and he applied the same things on the other aspects of his life. Friends, Amitabh Bachchan Sahab said a famous line that 'those who try are never defeated'. A lot of people do not agree to this point, because they accept an exam as the final decision of success and failure. Life is bigger than a test and a person trying towards his goal never gets failure and defeat. Pradeep believes that a person must pay attention to the aspects that are in his hands. Unnecessary worries hamper and impede us from our target, it also brings about trouble and stress in life, so try, fall, rise again, try again,

Because- 'Only the person making an effort gets success and failure.

One who is unable to muster the courage would neither rise nor fall'.

❑❑

12

Name: Jay Shivani
Rank: 81, CSE-2018

For this examination consistency, patience and perseverance are most important and we should try to just focus on the process and not the result.

JAY SHIVANI

OPTIONAL SUBJECT
Mathematics

MEDIUM
English

NATIVE PLACE
Bhopal (M.P.)

EDUCATIONAL QUALIFICATION
❖ B. Tech. in Computer Science and Engineering from IIT(ISM), Dhanbad

PARENTS' OCCUPATION
Father and elder brother into business, younger sister pursuing MBBS from KLE, Belgaum

COACHING TAKEN
None, Joined only test series

MARKS
Prelims: Paper -1: 106.66 and Paper -2: 168.33

MAINS MARKS AND PERSONALITY TEST
Essay (Paper I): 117
General Studies- I (Paper II): 96
General Studies- II (Paper III): 104
General Studies- III (Paper IV): 98
General Studies- IV (Paper V): 103
Optional - (Mathematics) (Paper I): 164
Optional - (Mathematics) (Paper II): 172
Written Total: 854
Personality Test: 171
Final Total: 1025

CONTACT OPTIONS

http://demystifycse.in/importance-of-choosing-right-optionaljay-shivani-air-81/#more-601

For more, I'll soon be coming up with my own blog.

Contact options (I'll try to revert as soon as possible):

Instagram: https://www.instagram.com/jayshivani/

Twitter: https://www.twitter.com/jayshivani7/

Facebook: https://www.facebook.com/jayshivani07/

MY JOURNEY

- This has been an awesome journey which started during later half of third year of my graduation. Appearing for this examination, or rather, becoming an IAS officer was in my mind from school days only but the only thing I knew about it was the word "IAS" and not even its full form properly. I didn't even know whether there is an examination for this or some different process. The thought was always there in the back of my mind but I started preparing for it seriously when I was in third year of my graduation after gaining a few experiences in service to the society through various opportunities I got during first two years of my college.
- Being in college I started preparing on my own. Relied on internet for initial guidance and even more on the seniors in college preparing for the examination. They had been a constant support in the whole journey and were available in any situation. Along with family, college seniors had been the major support.
- Like almost all the aspirants I too faced a lot of challenging situations and phases of extreme downs. Everyone has to overcome those situations and come out stronger.
- The most toughest been the whole one month before mains and even during mains in the last attempt when I was suffering from extreme wrist tendonitis. Was unable to write even one answer for the whole month and spent 1.5 hours daily with the physiotherapist for the whole month just before mains and during it too. Then too tried to give it my all and fortunately qualifying mains in that attempt gave me immense confidence and proved to me the importance of perseverance in this process.

- Regarding the choice of optional subject, I started thinking about the optional subject around Feb-March 2016. I was considering various optionals that can be looked into so as to choose one. Having no previous knowledge or experience in this preparation I went ahead with the general trend/myth of not even considering mathematics or science subjects even in the first shortlist. Even after having interest as well as confidence of doing well in science subjects I went ahead with downsizing my first shortlist without mathematics in it and my pen stopped at economics.
- After spending around 4-5 months in it and wasting around 6 months(from optional point of view as the knowledge gained is never wasted) because of this step I had to reconsider my options and finally boil down to mathematics in my final year.
- Due to this I was not able to give my best in mathematics in the limited time I was left with before my first attempt. Though I cleared mains in that attempt fortunately on the back of essay and GS, I missed the final list by around 25 marks. Mathematics score being very low of 252 in that attempt (increased to 336 in this attempt).
- In all what I would like to say is that before deciding to opt for a subject or before believing in any of the myths related to this examination consider all the factors, viz, your interest, your comfort with that decision, availability of material, scoring potential of that subject "for you personally", and the self-confidence you feel when you think about that decision.

MESSAGE TO NEW COMERS

- I've always believed that for this examination consistency, patience and perseverance are most important and we have to try to just focus on the process and not the result.
- Just keep enjoying the journey as it is the journey that will mould your personality and make you suitable for being recommended to be trained to become a civil servant.
- It is the journey which is more enjoyable and important than the destination. It'll will teach you a lot, not only from exam point of view but also for life in general.

- No external motivation will be needed if we have the right reason and intentions to pursue this career path, deciding to appear for this examination.
- For students still in their under graduation(or even for school students these days), do not try and indulge into this preparation too early so that your peak comes very much before even your first attempt. Try to keep your experiences diversified, pursue your hobbies and interests and grab the extra-curricular opportunities you get. This will even develop your personality very well.
- Come the right time tilt your priorities fully towards preparation and peak at the right time.
- Making targets and following schedules helps a lot.
- In all after taking a decision to appear for this examination with right reason and intentions, go through the syllabus very well. Read all the basic standard textbooks, follow newspapers and current affairs regularly and focus majorly on answer writing. Along with this choosing right optional and working nicely towards it is really important.

❑❑

13

Name: Nidhi Siwach
Rank: AIR- 83, CSE-2018

"खुदी को कर बुलंद इतना हर तक़दीर से पहले, खुदा बन्दे से खुद पूछे बता तेरी रज़ा क्या है।"

NIDHI SIWACH

OPTIONAL SUBJECT
History

MEDIUM
English

NATIVE PLACE
Gurugram, Haryana

EDUCATIONAL QUALIFICATION
❖ B.Tech (Mechanical engineering)

PARENTS' OCCUPATION
❖ **Father:** Shopkeeper (runs a general store)
❖ **Mother:** Homemaker

WORK EXPERIENCE
2 years as Design Engineer

MARKS
Prelims: GS 101.33, CSAT- 126

MAINS MARKS AND PERSONALITY TEST
Essay (Paper I): 129
General Studies- I (Paper II): 112
General Studies- II (Paper III): 107
General Studies- III (Paper IV): 096
General Studies- IV (Paper V): 122
Optional - (History) (Paper I): 150
Optional - (History) (Paper II): 140
Interview: 168, Final Total: 1024

CONTACT
Telegram: Born_fighter

MY JOURNEY

Sometimes, you don't choose the goal , but the goal chooses you. My story has a great similarity with this, I had chosen some other goal, but destiny and my mother wanted something else. People always say that there is a great role of a woman behind a successful man. But behind a successful daughter, her mother plays a vital role. A mother is like a potter who has to hit from outside while making the pot, but he also gives support by putting his hand in the pot from inside to make it flawless.

I was born in Bhani Surjan, a small village in Haryana where girl's education was not given due importance and even today this situation persists. Our ancestral patriarchal ideology and the importance of male dominance still exist in my village. My parents were literate. But under the pressure of my grandmother my father had to leave his job and started farming. My father had adopted that life but my mother had not. A mother giving birth to a girl child is not valued and respected in male dominated society and if she gives birth to two daughters, then her destiny is considered to be the worst. If all the mothers of a daughter learn the skill of tolerating the taunts and raise their voices and fight for their daughter then this conservative and orthodox society and its attitude can be transformed, otherwise these evils will continue swallow the lives of several girls. On this moment several persons congratulated and contacted me but I ascribe my all success to my mother and her harsh decisions. My mother knew the value of studies, so when I was four years old, she sent to my aunt residing at Faridabad so that I could study well without any disturbance. The story does not end here because there was also the question of my siblings along with me. My parents decided to leave the village and settle in Gurgaon and opened a shop. After completing the fifth standard I returned to my mother and father. When I got a chance to choose my career I opted for mechanical engineering but everyone did not accept my choice as the say that mechanical engineering is not considered good for girls, then some others said it is very difficult to study and she will not be able to pass. But there are some people in our society whose ideology is totally different. He suggested that the girl has completed 12th standard and she looks good, she has a good height and the money will you spend on her studies you can complete her marriage ceremony within it. If the girl receives higher education you will have to pay the huge amount of dowry and you have to marry your two daughters. My mother has not listened to any of these regressive ideas and supported me fully to continue further.

At the time of graduation, one thing was understood that the problem is not just to get education. Even after that you will have to fight for your rights. Core companies of mechanical engineering careers did not allow the girls in the campus placements and when asked for the reasons, they got silent. But if I want to speak in one word, I will call it the male dominance in society. After graduation my mother wanted me to prepare for civil services but my father's and my opinion was same to become independent. So I started a job in designing at TechMahindra, but I was not satisfied with this. I took the Air Force exam and its SSB gave a new direction to my life. At the time of interview in SSB, the interviewer suggested that I should focus on civil exams and from the academy encouraged me to fill up the form for the 2016 exam. I appeared in the first attempt without preparation but it increased my confidence and morale and that I could do it. With the job, I prepared for the 2016 exam. But due to the tasks assigned me on the job , I could not complete my prelims syllabus.

After the prelims of 2017, my father wanted to get me married, while I wanted to leave the job and focus with total attention on civil exam. It took me a week to convince my father while my mother did not speak this time too. But before leaving the job, my father put a condition that an attempt means only one attempt, whenever you got out of this exam at any of the stage whether prelims, mains or interview you will not refuse marriage after that. I just wanted a chance. I agreed to my father's condition. It is not his fault but our society is like this. When I left my job and came home, some people again came to my father and began to say that tell the girl to continue the job otherwise it will be difficult to get a suitable boy for marriage. I have a question, why after all, everything in a girl's life is linked to a boy and a marriage? Despite all these disturbances, I just focused on my studies because I had no time as I had to appear in the prelims on 3 June 2018 and everyone was talking about my marriage and all like the boys to with whom the issue of marriage is going on. But my dream was something else. I could not study for two weeks in this ambience. Finally my father agreed. After prelims, nobody was going to comment and bother me with these marriage related conversation. My mother and father did not let pass any matter to me and dealt with it themselves. People say that God does not give anything without examination, he is probably going to examine me. The biggest hindrance in that exam came in my first paper of Mains. On 24 September my first mains had an essay paper, half an hour had passed and I made a structure for my essay started writing the essay. I had written 2 pages and the boy sitting on the seat behind me accidentally spilled water on me. I was drenched and my entire answer sheet was soaked in water. On the worry of the water soaking the answer sheet, my good sense abandoned me. Thankfully, the examiner dried the sheets and it took me 10 minutes to recover myself and after wasting half an hour and I started writing again. At that time there was an extreme fear in my mind, hands were also trembling, but one thing dominated my mind, that if this opportunity gets out of hand, do you ever know if you will get this opportunity or not? Somehow I finished my paper.

After coming home, I woke my sleeping mother and told her about the near devastating incident during the exam. She said, my child, it is very easy to break down and emotion dominates many times, but when the pressure is on peak, then understand that it is going to end soon. It is the darkest before dawn, so just keep doing your work and what has happened is done. Do not spoil tomorrow.

Because of these words of assurance from my mother, I wrote the rest of my papers and the result changed my whole life. This is not just my story, this is the story of every other girl in our country. I would like to say from my experience that everything is not available easily, you have to fight if you want to get anything, you will also have to work hard and there will be many occasions when you will find yourself alone against everyone. Do not bow down and break even in juncture. This world will stand before you, if you will not bow down.

"Khudi ko kar buland itna ke har taqder se pehle Khuda bande se khud pooche bata teri raza kya hai"

MESSAGE FOR NEWCOMERS

From my experience, I would request you to

- Prioritize things and fight back if you want to achieve your dream, not everyone is going to support you.
- You have your plans but destiny has its own. You can change destiny if you don't lose control over your senses and emotions. This will be best judged during prelims exams as its most unpredictable. So be prepared to face it with control over your senses and sail through with flying colors.

- Coaching is not necessary and you can crack it without coaching and without study groups too. Just you have to put in little more efforts.

STUDY PLAN

I used to study limited things but focused more on revision and making short notes so that I am able to revise it in last one week before exam. I would suggest you to

- keeping sources limited
- practice more and more
- refer to previous year question papers
- making short notes
- attempting mock tests and then checking the model answers as well as toppers copies of the same test to check what better they did
- focusing on mistakes and not the marks that I am getting
- UPSC is not just an exam it's a journey which will change your thought process, how you perceive the things and your outlook towards the world. But be selective while studying you need to qualify the exam not top in it. Give focus on your goal and be optimistic. Remember it's easy to bear the burden of discipline than bearing the burden of regret of not giving your best and failure.

❑❑

14

Name: Abhishek Jain
Rank: 111

"Success is a journey not a destination. The doing is often more important than the outcome".

ABHISHEK JAIN

OPTIONAL SUBJECT
Commerce & Accountancy

MEDIUM
English

NATIVE PLACE
Rohini, Delhi

EDUCATIONAL QUALIFICATION
- B.COM (Hons.) from Hansraj college, Delhi University

PARENTS' OCCUPATION
- **Father:** Businessman
- **Mother:** Homemaker

MARKS
Prelims: Paper -1: 108 and Paper -2: 117

MAINS MARKS AND PERSONALITY TEST
Essay (Paper I): 127
General Studies- I (Paper II): 097
General Studies- II (Paper III): 117
General Studies- III (Paper IV): 121
General Studies- IV (Paper V): 104
Optional - (Commerce & Accountancy) (Paper I): 139
Optional - (Commerce & Accountancy) (Paper II): 132
Interview: 179
Final Total: 1016

MY JOURNEY

- My grandfather is a retired government officer. He has worked with several civil servants during his career and used to tell me how they took several important decisions concerning the welfare of the people. These stories developed a strong desire to become a civil servant in me.
- I had started reading NCERT books during my college. But I started my preparation in a full fledged way just after my graduation.
- To begin with, I watched lots of topper talks on youtube to gain an insight into the various strategies followed by the successful candidates. Taking inputs from them, I developed my own strategy and timetable and then followed it religiously. Further, I practiced several test papers. The exam days were, without a doubt, stressful. But I had realized that UPSC is not just a test of our hard work & knowledge but also our **temperament** and **mental strength.** Thus, I tried to remain positive during the exam.
- It feels really great when your hard work pays off. The HOLY PDF filled me with sheer joy and excitement. I had cleared the exam in my 1st attempt ! I cannot even describe the happiness of my family. The days ahead were going to be exciting. As I looked into the past, all those late night studies, last time revisions, multiple tests, notes, frustrations, ups and downs, all of them .....WERE WORTH IT.

MESSAGE FOR NEWCOMERS

- "Success is a journey not a destination. The doing is often more important than the outcome". UPSC is a long and arduous exam. There are bound to be good and bad phases during this process. But the need is to enjoy this journey and learn from your mistakes at each step.
- Hard work and dedication have no substitutes. But by complementing them with a smart strategy which is aligned with demands of the exam is the best way forward.
- In the end, UPSC is another exam after all. It is not the end of the world. Thus, it should be treated that way so as to avoid undue stress which negatively affects your performance.
- You have chosen to take the leap forward and write this exam. So you are already a winner! I wish you best of luck and assure you that it will all be worth it!

❑❑❑

15

Name: Atul Kumar Bansal
Rank: AIR 115, Civil Services Exam 2018

"A balanced preparation, frequent revision and lots of practice, that's the key to succeed."

ATUL KUMAR BANSAL

OPTIONAL SUBJECT
History

MEDIUM
English

NATIVE PLACE
Padampur, District - Sriganganagar, Rajasthan

EDUCATIONAL QUALIFICATION
- B.Tech in Mechanical Enginnering from IIT Roorkee

PARENTS' OCCUPATION
- **Father:** Advocate
- **Mother:** Teacher

COACHING / SELF STUDY
Coaching taken for some part, some part covered by self study. Even if opting for coaching, one should rely upon self study only.

MARKS
Prelims: Paper -1: 107.34 and Paper -161.68

MAINS MARKS AND PERSONALITY TEST
Essay (Paper I): 132
General Studies- I (Paper II): 101
General Studies- II (Paper III): 113
General Studies- III (Paper IV): 109
General Studies- IV (Paper V): 094
Optional - (History) (Paper I): 139
Optional - (History) (Paper II): 154
Total: 842
Interview: 173
Final Total: 1015

MY JOURNEY

(a) Struggle

I first came to know about Civil Services while I was working as Scientist 'SC' in the Indian Space Research Organization. Some of my friends were preparing for this exam and it was after talking with them, did I gain an insight into Civil Services Preparation, different civil services, job prospects etc. Out of curiosity, I read about the pioneering work being done by some IAS officers like Daliya Jalao Abhiyan etc. I started thinking about Civil Services Preparation seriously by end of 2014 as it offered unique opportunity to grow personally and professionally, as well as make oneself more useful to society. I also realized that I would not be able to do justice to my Civil Services Preparation and my job simultaneously. I left my job in the beginning of 2015. So began – 'my civil services journey'.

My journey is not full of difficulties and sufferings but it certainly is unique. I came to Old Rajendra Nagar in New Delhi which is the pilgrimage of all aspirants. Without much preparation, I gave an attempt in 2015 but failed to clear Prelims stage. I appeared next year with full preparation, cleared Prelims of CSE 2016 with a good score, but couldn't clear the Mains. Lack of sufficient answer writing practice and weak current affairs preparation was the reason behind it.

So I prepared next year. I left no stone unturned in my preparation. I appeared for CSE 2017 Mains with full preparation. Tried again, failed again.

That was the first real failure of my life. It was the lowest point I have faced in my life till now. I had prepared whole-heartedly and had failed. I panicked on one particular exam day and ruined my GS3 and GS4 paper. Despite good scores in all other subjects, I had failed to make it to the interview.

I went home as I could barely live by myself in that depressing environment. For the next 20 days, I stayed at home. I don't know how my parents bore me. I was practically a living dead in those days. I barely spoke a word for the whole day. I could hardly see anyone eye to eye. My confidence had hit rock bottom. I knew I had to get out of that mess.

With all the energy left in me, I started preparing once again. I promised to myself that I would not be that miserable ever again. I came to Delhi and carefully analyzed each and every question asked in CSE 2017 Mains and where

I could have improved. I went through each and every word of the syllabus, downloaded countless topper's copies, kept my copies of Vision IAS test series side by side topper's copies and carefully analyzed each answer written by me. I had never seen myself so disciplined. Prelims was not a problem as I have been clearing it easily. Mains was the real problem and I gave my 100% for it. The result came on 22 December, 2018. I had cleared it. I appeared for an interview and finally made it to the coveted list with AIR 115.

Looking back, I see this journey as something which was full of highs and lows, pleasure and pain, but it was certainly transformational. It taught me to be hardworking, disciplined, positive and patient. Throughout my preparation, I used to remember these lines to keep myself motivated:

वृक्ष हों भले खड़े,

हों घने हों बड़े,

एक पत्र छाँह भी,

माँग मत, माँग मत, माँग मत,

-- अग्निपथ

(b) List of Books

- History
  - (a) **Ancient India:** Old NCERT by R.S. Sharma
  - (b) **Medieval India:** New NCERT
  - (c) **Modern India:** Old NCERT by Bipin Chandra + Spectrum
  - (d) **World History:** Old NCERT by Arjun Dev
- Art and Culture
  - (a) An Introduction to Indian Art: Class 11 NCERT
  - (b) CCRT Notes
- Society
  - (a) Class 12 NCERTs (2 books)
- Geography
  - (a) New NCERTs of Class 11 and 12
  - (b) Mrunal Lectures on geography by Rajtanil Mam (available on youtube)

- Polity and Governance
  - (a) Class 11 NCERT - Indian Constitution at work
  - (b) Laxmikant for Prelims
  - (c) Took classes at M.Puri's IAS and referred class notes
- **International Relations**
  - (a) Class 12 NCERT - Contemporary world politics
- **Economy**
  - (a) Indian Economic Development
  - (b) Sriram's notes
- **Environment**
  - (a) Shankar IAS Academy notes
- **Internal Security**
  - (a) Sriram's IAS notes
- **Ethics**
  - (a) Took Pawan Kumar Sir's classes. And referred the class notes.
  - (b) Lexicon - not to be read word by word but can be referred for seeing definition of different terms

Current Affairs

- One national newspaper like The Hindu, Indian Express
- Monthly Current Affairs magazines of VisionIAS for Mains related topics. Current affairs compilation VisionIAS PT 365 for Prelims.
- RSTV Big Picture Debates - especially good for International Relations part in GS Paper 2.

Government Documents to be read

- Economic Survey
- Union Budget
- Yojana Magazine
- NITI Aayog - Three-year action agenda.

Answer Writing

- I did daily answer writing practice at TLP IAS Baba. Joined Vision IAS test series. For History Optional, I joined Self-Study History test series.

(c) History Optional Strategy

History as an optional is decently scoring although the possibility of getting too high scores like 320+ is very less. For history optional, I took classes (Baliyan Sir) as I was not having any previous background in the subject. But many aspirants do manage by self-study also.

For optional, I would recommend not to read too many books as it would compromise your general-studies preparation. Here is a list of books I referred:

- **Ancient India:** Old NCERT by R.S.Sharma, class notes, Upinder Singh
- **Medieval India:** Old NCERT by Satish Chandra, class notes, IGNOU notes
- **Modern India:** Old NCERT by Bipin Chandra, class notes, Grover and Mehta, Spectrum, few chapters from Plassey to Partition
- **World History:** Old NCERT by Arjun Dev, class notes, Norman Lowe, L. Mukherjee.

Most of these books are to be read completely but still if you refer the UPSC syllabus, you will find some of the topics can be skipped which are not in the syllabus.

Along with reading the books, I would recommend that you **make small, bullet point notes for last time revision.**

Other than this, **Map** in an important part which should not be ignored.

Keep referring to previous year question papers. It helps in knowing which part of the syllabus is more important. Many of the questions do repeat also.

Answer writing is another important aspect. Join a good test series. You can do daily answer writing practice also. Some of the portals like *Self Study History, IAS baba* have programs for daily answer writing practice. Writing past years' questions is best way for daily answer writing practice.

MESSAGE FOR NEW COMERS

UPSC CSE can very well be cleared by any serious aspirant. Those of us who fail, it's because we commit some mistakes. Based upon my experience with CSE preparation, I would like to share few tips with you which might help you to clear the exam:

Points to be noted

- ❖ The booklist is merely indicative and not exhaustive. If you have referred to some other books/notes and find it useful, please follow it.
- ❖ For some of the topics like International Relations, Paper 3 topics, etc. there is no standard booklist. They are to be covered from current affairs part.
- ❖ Some of the topics like World History, Physical Geography, Medieval Indian History, etc. have a low **cost-benefit ratio.** The weight of questions asked from them is not substantial. So do not spend too much time preparing for them.
- ❖ This is an integrated list for both Prelims and Mains. For those who are just starting with preparation, they should first go through these books/ notes first. Then preparation specific to prelims can be started 3–4 months before the prelims exam.

1. Your main focus of preparation should be Mains. Give 3–4 months to Prelims preparation before Prelims exam.
2. Keep a balance between GS preparation and Optional. Give adequate time to all GS papers.
3. Do not ignore essay and ethics paper.
4. Choose your Optional carefully as it can be a deciding factor.
5. Do a lot of answer writing practice. Answer writing practice consists of daily answer writing and test series.
6. Read one good newspaper religiously.
7. If possible, try to cover Rajya Sabha Big Picture debates. They would help you to develop perspective and argumentation skills.
8. Watch few toppers' talk videos on YouTube. Learn about their strategy and book list.
9. Don't ignore NCERTs, especially Class 11th and 12th NCERTs.
10. Make notes of all the topics that you cover.
11. Keep referring to syllabus and previous years question papers regularly.
12. For **Prelims:** Try to develop the art of eliminating options/ making intelligent guesses/ using common sense to arrive at an answer. It would prove very useful.
13. For **Mains:** try to attempt as much questions as possible and draw relevant diagrams, flow charts wherever necessary. Write in bullet points in GS answers.

❑❑

16

Name: Manish Meena
Rank: 144 (ST RANK 1), CSE, 2018

"There is no shortcut, what is needed is Consistency, Dedication, Smart Work, and Time Management."

MANISH MEENA

OPTIONAL SUBJECT
Political Science and International Relations

MEDIUM
English

NATIVE PLACE
Jaipur

EDUCATIONAL QUALIFICATION
- B.Tech. Electrical Engineering from IIT Bombay (2017)

PARENTS' OCCUPATION
- Father: Banker
- Mother: Teacher

COACHING TAKEN
Vajiram and Ravi for GS, No coaching for optional subject

MAINS MARKS AND PERSONALITY TEST
Essay (Paper I): 112
General Studies- I (Paper II): 091
General Studies- II (Paper III): 104
General Studies- III (Paper IV): 107
General Studies- IV (Paper V): 098
Optional - (Political Science and Int. Relations) (Paper I): 148
Optional - (Political Science and Int. Relations) (Paper II): 156
Total: 816
Interview: 193
Final Total: 1009

MY JOURNEY

I was never one of those who plan their life well in advance. I had no plans of becoming a civil servant until 4th year of my college. In my 4th year, I started thinking about my future prospects and civil services appeared to be a good option. During this time, I started reading newspapers more seriously and overtime, the desire for public service inside me grew.

Consequently, after getting out of college, I chose to prepare for civil services rather than going for a job in private sector. I took GS coaching classes in Vajiram and Ravi to kickstart my preparation. At that time, I was not clear about my optional subject which I finalized only after 2 months.

I started with the static portions of the course and first covered all the required NCERTs. As soon as I had finalized my optional subject, I bought Shubhra Ranjan Madam's notes for PSIR. My goal was to go through the entire course as quickly as possible in the 1st reading to get a sense of the things that I had to cover so that I could plan my studies accordingly. I made a timeline of what portion of what course I had to cover and when, which sometimes I couldn't follow but it helped me monitor my progress and keep me on track, which is very important. After 2 readings of its course, I joined optional test series in GS Score in Oct'17 which got over by Feb'18. Joining this test series was a good decision, it helped me practice answer writing as well as prepare material for mains and most importantly memorize important things.

Up until March, I was preparing the entire material keeping mains exam in mind, it was only in April that I started preparing exclusively for Prelims, so I had 2 months for that (though I would recommend giving 3 months exclusively for Prelims exam preparation).

As is the case with almost everyone, there were times when this whole task seemed too huge and impossible to achieve, but it is exactly in these moments that your mental strength is tested so it is important to keep going. It is also very usual to get bored during this long journey, so I would say that some kind of entertainment is necessary to relax.

After prelims, I joined a GS mains test series (Byju's), but I did not join any optional test series this time. Preparing for Mains is a little different from Prelims. For mains, it is possible for us to go for selective reading as it is more predictable than prelims. It is very important to go for smart work rather than 'brute force-hard work'. Test series is of utmost importance in the preparation for mains.

For Personality Test, I prepared my DAF, state, graduation stream, and read 2 newspapers daily (Indian Express and The Hindu). This phase of exam is more about preparing yourself mentally for the interview rather than acquiring lots and lots of knowledge. Joining a few mock interviews really helps in refining your way of answering and overall personality.

The result was a surprise because I did not expect this in my 1st attempt. After this long and tiring journey, and all the time and effort I put into the preparation, it really felt like a blessing.

LIST OF BOOKS

❖ **For General Science:** The following video gives a decent guide for the various sources to be referred: *https://www.youtube.com/watch?v=_eAuJstb2zE*

(a) Sources that I referred

(i) Newspaper + Vajiram Notes + VisionIAS monthly Current Affair magazines

(ii) Modern History: Spectrum*

(iii) World History: 11th, 12th old Ncerts

(iv) Ancient History/Art and Culture: Ncert + TN board 11th book+ CCRT website

(v) Post-Independence History: Selected topics from Bipin Chandra

(vi) Polity: Laxmikanth*

(vii) Economics: Ncert + Eco. Survey + Budget

(viii) Geography: Ncert

(ix) Environment: current affairs + last 4 chapters of Bio Ncert

(x) Governance: current affairs

(xi) IR: newspapers

(xii) Disaster Management: current affairs

(xiii) Science and Tech: current affairs

(xiv) Ethics: Lexicon

(xv) Any other topic left was covered from newspaper and other current affairs

(xvi) RSTV programs on Youtube: The Big Picture and India's World

❖ **For optional:** I read Shubhra Madam's notes for static portions and took help from test series and internet whenever I felt like. For International Relations, I read newspapers, a few blogs of well-known IR commentators, followed Gateway House think tank and made my own notes accordingly.

MESSAGE FOR NEWCOMERS

There is no shortcut, what is needed is Consistency, Dedication, Smart Work, and Time Management. Have faith in yourselves. Do not let some failures to adversely affect your preparation.

As far as books are concerned, it is very very important to avoid multiple sources for a single topic unless it is absolutely necessary. Go for qualitative learning, try to keep the number of sources to minimum while ensuring that you cover entire syllabus.

Also keep in touch with 3-4 people who are preparing for exam seriously. This would help you stay on course and not read something unnecessarily. A note of caution would be to never copy someone else's strategy. Talk to a few people and make your own strategy. Keep your preparation dynamic, adjusting it whenever required. Remember,

"It's not how much you want it, it's how much you work for it that matters"

❑❑

17

Name: Dr. Pooja Gupta
Rank: AIR- 147, CSE-2018

"UPSC CSE is not just an exam but a process that put to test our physical and mental strength. The goal is to maintain our mental calm through the whole process."

DR. POOJA GUPTA

OPTIONAL SUBJECT
Anthropology

MEDIUM
English

NATIVE PLACE
Trinagar, Delhi

EDUCATIONAL QUALIFICATION
❖ Bachelor of Dental Surgery [BDS]

PARENTS' OCCUPATION
❖ **Father:** Private employee
❖ **Mother:** Delhi Police

COACHING TAKEN
GS: KSG Delhi

MARKS
Prelims: Paper -1: 104 **and Paper -2:** 115

MAINS MARKS AND PERSONALITY TEST
Essay (Paper I): 127
General Studies- I (Paper II): 95
General Studies- II (Paper III): 90
General Studies- III (Paper IV): 107
General Studies- IV (Paper V): 111
Optional - (Anthropology) (Paper I): 165
Optional - (Anthropology) (Paper II): 171
Written Total: 866
Personality Test: 143
Final Total: 1009

MY JOURNEY

(a) The Exam

UPSC CSE is not just an exam but a process that puts to test our physical and mental strength. The goal is to maintain our mental calm through the whole process.

Prelims

It was my very first attempt for UPSC CSE, so time and again I was highly anxious about my direction of preparation. Prelims was very tough that year. There was uncertainty about the cut off. I was not sure whether to start preparation for mains or not.

Days passed, I mustered all my courage and reassured myself that I had put my 100% for prelims, so its time to start preparation for mains. So the moral here is no matter what TRUST YOURSELF AND YOUR HARD WORK!!

Mains

The journey through mains is more strenuous. Practice is the key to mains. I focused extensively on writing practice and that helped me to sail through mains. RELIGIOUSLY follow your deadlines, prepare your timetable and don't miss even a single test.

(b) Book List

The basic books remains the same, some sources that I found to be very good are

- Hind Swaraj by MK Gandhi
- Freedom Battle by MK Gandhi
- The story of my experiments with truth by MK Gandhi

Other Study Sources

https://mrunal.org/ ❖ *https://www.insightsactivelearn.com/*

❖ *http://pib.nic.in/* ❖ *https://www.prsindia.org/*

❑❑

18

Name: Ram Niwas Bugalia
Rank: 159, CSE, 2018

"UPSC is definitely tough but its not insurmountable, be optimistic and give your best".

RAM NIWAS BUGALIA

OPTIONAL SUBJECT
Anthropology

MEDIUM
English

NATIVE PLACE
Sudrasan, Tehsil- Didwana, Nagaur, Rajasthan

EDUCATIONAL QUALIFICATION
- M.Tech (Information and Communication Engineering)

WORK EXPERIENCE
United India Insurance (April 2014) Income Tax Inspector

PARENTS' OCCUPATION
- Father: Teacher
- Mother: Homemaker

MARKS
Prelims: GS 115.34; CSAT 115.83

MAINS MARKS AND PERSONALITY TEST
Essay (Paper I): 116
General Studies- I (Paper II): 101
General Studies- II (Paper III): 101
General Studies- III (Paper IV): 104
General Studies- IV (Paper V): 104
Optional - (Anthropology) (Paper VI): 167
Optional - (Anthropology) (Paper VII): 160
Written Total: 853
Personality Test: 154
Final Total: 1007

MY JOURNEY

Struggle Part/UPSC Journey Part

"The destination will be found right by wandering,

Misguided are those who do not come out of the house".

The destination is easy to set, but it is equally difficult to walk on its path. Many people start their journey in search of a destination but on the way where they find tranquility and satisfaction, they consider it his own goal and destination. My story is also something like this, in which it had many twists and halts but I considered them as a night shelter and did not miss the right goal and finally I got it too.

After completing my post graduation in information and communication technology in 2013 I proceeded to move towards my goal (IAS). But my way to achieve this tremendous goal was quite different, which was largely a result of the then circumstances. I had achieved my final goal but it was important to be self-reliant, so I started this journey like climbing the stairs, where many stops come but the last destination is IAS. Along with studying for my civil services exams, I also started taking other jobs.

I was selected as an Administrative Officer at United India Insurance in April 2014 which I have joined. I continued with UPSC studies and in August 2014 appeared in prelims. This prelims made me realize that I still have to work hard to achieve my destination.

The caravan kept changing as the journey continued. I assumed the responsibility of income tax inspector after the job in insurance. Getting out of these journey, I covered the distance of IAS from RAS. There were also some places, where I could stay for a lifetime, but I wish to get the ultimate goal. While working, many times I felt like quitting the job, feeling the pressure of the exam to let what is going on affect me. The key is to manage everything well in this juncture you will surely get to your goal and if you do not handle it well then you will make this halt as your final destination.

This journey of mine has been like a ladder where I achieved everything gradually. It took a slightly long time but gave the immense satisfaction, as the dreaming of the journey from earth to sky gets somewhat fearful and doubtful, but every time there were stops, I was on the path of progress and my morale always remained and kept me motivated to work hard. If the journey is hard but performed with someone then it gets easier. Many people helped me in this journey. My family's co-operation and support boosted my morale a lot and after this where I was posted, my seniors and friends also supported me fully.

From my UPSC experience, the only advice I would like to give is that whatever the difficulties you will have to face on your path in achieving your goal, don't look behind and work towards your goal with full might. If you have the courage to cover the goal, then try your best to achieve it. In achieving this toughest goal you might have to face a lot of difficulties and disappointments. But after going through all this hardship, when you achieve your destination, then it will be the matter of utmost happiness, joy and satisfaction.

MESSAGE FOR NEWCOMERS

UPSC CSE is a competitive exam and to be in the competition one should get feel of it and remain in touch with reality. Based on my experience of 3 mains and 2 selections, I would like to suggest:

- ❖ Do writing practice, write mock tests and get them evaluated. You are competing against lakhs of brilliant minds. One mistake and you need to start afresh. Don't go with casual attitude, "Ho jayega.. It needs efforts. "
- ❖ Keep reading newspapers. I couldn't keep track of it during my 2017 attempt and it reflected in my AIR 794, so newspapers are the best source but don't be biased, try to take a holistic view.
- ❖ Focus on the presentation part. Evaluator evaluates nearly 60-70 copies per day what's so special that he should give you marks? Its the presentation part and innovative writing which will encourage evaluator to give you more marks. For reference, you can go through Anudeep Durishetty's strategy. Try to incorporate diagrams, flowcharts, tables and maps wherever possible.

Study Plan

Study plan will vary from person to person depending on their strengths and weaknesses. Some students are blessed with good writing skills while some are good in memorizing facts. So, students should know their weaknesses and strengths and then plan accordingly.

- ❖ Devote time to all subjects equally but essay and optional shouldn't be ignored at any cost.
- ❖ For working candidates, they need to prioritize the topics and prepare accordingly, given the paucity of time
- ❖ Focuse on quality of material and areas covered not too much on quantity
- ❖ Focuse basic concepts because trend is shifting towards analytical questions which checks the basic understanding of a candidate

All the very best to all the candidates.

❑❑

19

Name: Dipankar Choudhary
Rank: 166, CSE-2018

This exam is not only a test of your academic abilities but is also a big test of your physical persistence and emotional stability. Clear your mind and stick to your basics, the success will be yours.

DIPANKAR CHOUDHARY

OPTIONAL SUBJECT
Public Administration

MEDIUM
English

NATIVE PLACE
Hazaribagh (Jharkhand)

EDUCATIONAL QUALIFICATION
❖ B.Tech – Delhi Technological university (DTU), 2015

PARENTS' OCCUPATION
❖ **Father:** Civil servant retd. (Joint secretary Govt of Jharkhand)
❖ **Mother:** Civil servant retd.

MAINS MARKS AND PERSONALITY TEST
Essay (Paper I): 126
General Studies- I (Paper II): 101
General Studies- II (Paper III): 110
General Studies- III (Paper IV): 108
General Studies- IV (Paper V): 097
Optional - I (Pub. Ad.) (Paper VI): 146
Optional - II (Pub. Ad.) (Paper VII): 156
Written Total: 844
Personality Test: 162
Final Total: 1006

MY JOURNEY IN BRIEF

I graduated in mathematics and computing from Delhi technological University in 2015. After my graduation, I was placed in an IT firm with a handsome salary package. Initially I was inclined towards it, however very soon I realized that my true ambition lay in civil services. By the end of 2015, I had made up my mind that I would go for civil services.

I did try and attempt in 2015 but that was bound to be an utter failure. After preparing for about 7-8 months, I wrote to preliminary exam of 2016. I failed in it.

Of course, this was a devastating experience, but I could pick up myself with relative ease and start my preparation again. In 2017 I managed to clear the preliminary exam. But this time I failed the main exam by six marks. This was a very devastating result for me. Though I could pick up myself with relative ease in 2016 but 2017 was a totally different experience. For me the world had come to a standstill. I did not know what to do, my job experience was very limited, I was not sure if I could ever clear this examination and I was at the verge of clinical depression. After spending about two years in the process I was nowhere. But I took inspiration from other people who had fought against worse odds and conquered the examinations.

Since the preliminary exam was not far away, I pulled myself together and started the preparation. Prelims has always been the diciest step of the entire process. The rate of success is very low, and luck plays a very important role here.

My preliminary exam was alright, but I was starting to doubt myself as I was standing somewhere at the border. This stage is even worse because you don't know if you should start preparing for the main examination. With a heavy heart I started with the main preparation. I felt as if I had conquered the world and the entire examination, the day they declared the prelims result.

However, the real fight still awaited me. I started my mains preparation by keeping in mind that I had to make every conscious effort in my answer writing so as to minimize the risk of any unfortunate happenings in the interview.

I read a lot of toppers answer sheets and looked at answer writing tricks and tips from them. I will briefly discuss them here

Answer writing: There are three aspects to your answer: the length of the answer, the content of the answer and the presentation of the answer. Their importance in the decreasing order is as follows: The presentation is more important than the content and the content is more important than the length. So, one should improve one's presentation by including flowcharts, diagrams, maps et cetera.

For content, one should have data and should always mention the legal side of an answer. By saying legal side, what I mean is articles of the Constitution, any laws which are applicable, Supreme Court judgements, or any commission report to support your argument.

The main exam in 2018: In GS1, I had messed up a few questions. This immediately brought me down before the next paper, but I managed to pull myself together and take my mind off from the mistakes I had already made. Optional was another challenge for me as I had always scored less in that. But this time I was confident because I had written enough test series and practiced enough number of questions. The main exam went alright, and I felt sure of clearing the examination, but I was never sure that I could land up in the final list.

The interview: I had good communication skills, so I was a bit confident for my interview. Still I took no chances and prepared every aspect of my DAF very diligently. The interview went on for about half an hour. I was very satisfied with the process.

Final thoughts: It took me four attempts to clear the exam. While at times it might seem that it is an endless tunnel, do remember that with hard work and dedication, there is always a light at the end of the tunnel.

MESSAGE FOR NEWCOMERS

This exam is not only a test of your academic abilities but is also a big test of your physical persistence and emotional stability. So while you prepare very hard for your academic success in this exam, make sure that it doesn't take a toll on your physical and emotional health. The process might seem long to you but trust me, as I've said, there is a light at the end of this tunnel and that is worth fighting for. Clear your mind and stick to your basics, the success will be yours.

❑❑

20

Name: Arpit Bohra
Rank: 178, CSE-2018

"Civil Service Exam is difficult and different from any other exam and it requires a lot of patience on part of an aspirant."

ARPIT BOHRA

OPTIONAL SUBJECT
Anthropology

MEDIUM
English

NATIVE PLACE
Chittorgarh Rajasthan

EDUCATIONAL QUALIFICATION
❖ Graduate in Civil engineering from Nirma University Ahmedabad (2015)

PARENTS' OCCUPATION
❖ **Father:** Assistant Accounts' Officer in State Government
❖ **Father:** Homemaker

COACHING TAKEN
❖ Yes

MARKS
Prelims: 104.66

MAINS MARKS AND PERSONALITY TEST
Essay (Paper I) : 140
General Studies- I (Paper II): 087
General Studies- II (Paper III) : 098
General Studies- III (Paper IV) : 103
General Studies- IV (Paper V) : 113
Optional - I (Anthropology) (Paper VI) : 147
Optional - II (Anthropology) (Paper VII) : 151
Written Total: 839
Personality Test: 165 ❖ **Final Total:** 1004

MY JOURNEY

For most of my preparation, I did self study. I took coaching in optional from Delhi and also joined a test series for mains exam in Delhi only. For GS part I think self study is sufficient and for most of the people who are not able to go to Delhi for any reason whatsoever, I can suggest that there is not much need of coaching in any part of the preparation (except test series of mains).

Today we have a huge resource of information available to us called as Internet and if utilised smartly you can do better than those who are taking coaching from expensive coaching in Delhi. (I am not against coaching as I myself took help of coaching materials which are available online or offline in Delhi).

My strategy, for exam was clear. I followed basic books approach and then build upon that. Books are suggested by many toppers so I will skip it to minimum at end but the thing is that you must stick yourselves to one concrete source and make notes from that. Notes are going to be important in your preparation, so make your own notes and do not depend on readymade material.

Exam is difficult and different from any other exam and it requires a lot of patience on part of an aspirant. I could not clear prelims in my first two attempts (although only second was serious) with small margins. The point that I want you to know that please don't get disheartened by result of preliminary exam as it has become more harder than ever, year by year in past three exams. Don't let others judge you or demotivate you. Believe me, success comes to those who wait for it. All a person can do is hard work and nothing else, so be sincere to that.

I used to study for 5-6 hours daily on average for prelims and 8-10 hours for mains (this figure can vary depending upon your preparation level and time you have for next attempt). Regularity is more important rather than studying more at single stretch. Keep a healthy routine, mind need, to relax for next stages and a marathon run.

I had left the job to give my full attention to UPSC. If one feels confident, he can do the same but if your situation doesn't allow you, make sure that a tight routine is to be followed very strictly without major lapses or the preparation itself can be take very long time and nothing would be achieved. While preparing full time, I had only a single minded will to focus on PSC's exam and nothing else (diverse focus is bad). For me leaving the job was a difficult decision as was from a service class family, I never had any backup (no business, no agriculture) and it was a huge risk as nobody can be sure in this exam. There were times that I felt low but kept myself motivated and worked hard, for that, I would suggest, prepare this exam in a group or make contact with people who have similar interests. Telegram app proved to be good help.

Some of the sources I referred:

- *Laxmikanth:* polity
- *Spectrum:* modern history
- *Tamil Nadu state board:* Ancient and medieval History
- *Shankar IAS:* Environment
- NCERT for everything else

The Hindu and Indian express and Vision IAS material for current affairs and issues.

Insights of India. PIB and PRS sometimes.

Mrunal videos for geography and econmics

Make topic wise notes of syllabus given by UPSC in General studies 2 and 3. Add content qualitatively by current issues. Always remember, basics must be strong. Its no use to focus on current issues spread over here and there.

A strong foundation is needed for making beautiful super structure. Current issues are like a cream on the cake, base is basics, which is main thing.

Finally remember ones and two's win a battle but to win a war, we need both, momentum and hard work.

❑❑

21

Name: Siddhartha Nahar
Rank: 182, CSE-2018

"Striving for success without hard work is like trying to harvest where you haven't planted."

SIDDHARTHA NAHAR

OPTIONAL SUBJECT
Philosophy

MEDIUM
English

NATIVE PLACE
Jodhpur

WORK-EXPERIENCE IF ANY
❖ 6 Years

Details of other competitive exams, including success/failures-
Not Appeared

COACHING
❖ 2 Month Coaching in Vajiram then Left

Service preferences (Top-5)
IFS>IAS>IPS>IRS(IT)>IRS(CE)>IAAS

Preference for the first states in top-3 zonal cadres.
Rajasthan, Gujarat, Karnataka

MY JOURNEY

I believe in doing unconventional things in life which pushed me to complete my undergraduate degree in Petroleum Engineering. After Graduation, I worked with GSPL as Procurement Officer for 2 years (2012-2014). While working, I got inspired by the working style of Tapan Ray Sir (IAS), who at that time was MD of GSPC Group. His vision of establishing online procurement in the company took shape very quickly. This made me realize the impact and changes an IAS officer can bring in a short amount of time. This incident inspired me to start preparing for this exam. While preparing for the Exam (2014-2018), I owned a small Online Education Business to finance myself during the preparation phase. In this, I sold software tutorials to my audience in the USA and Australia.

My Family belongs to Jodhpur (Rajasthan). My father is an Engineer and works as a Construction Consultant while my mother is a Homemaker. My Wife, Divya is a Chartered Accountant (CA) and owns a consultancy Firm.

I did not have much struggle with this work because I loved my work and I loved studying. So, I was able to manage both of them. It's not that there were no problems but if you love what you do, then all the problems can be overcome.

I had given my first 2 attempts in 2015-2016 but without any serious preparation. After my marriage, my wife convinced me to give the exam again and she stood by me during those 2 years of preparation and exam. There was no need to get back to UPSC but she made me realize that I had left something without completing it and I need to go back and do it. That kept me motivated. My Father, Mother and Brother had a much greater role. I had not told about my preparation to anyone except these 4 people in my life. So, they played a great role in keeping my preparation a secret from family and friends. It was not like I did not want to tell anyone but I did not want unnecessary social pressure on me. I was living a double life for 2 years and these 4 people were the ones who helped me through that tough time.

Having mood swings and distraction was a regular phenomenon for me. It was difficult to handle it alone, so I shifted from Gurgaon (My work place) to Jodhpur (My Home Town) so that I can be with family. This really helped me a lot. Other things I did were:

- Reminded myself everyday Why was I doing it
- Learnt that mood swings are only temporary but my achievements will bring long term results
- The weirdest thing I did was Watching Dark Thriller and Crime Thrillers on Netflix. When I finished watching them, I realized my life is so easy and simple. All I have to do is sit and study. That seemed like an easier task. I hope you get the idea.
- Planned short 2-3 days' vacation with my wife every 3rd month. Trust me, small vacations help you a lot.
- Pursuit of Happiness is my favourite movie. I always thought, If Chris Gardner can make it happen despite all odds, I can also do it.

Prelim and final mark sheet:

Subjects (Max. Marks)	Marks secured	Cutoff ranges (PH to Gen.)
Prelims P1-GS (200m)	102	Cutoff: 40-98
Prelims P2-Aptitude (200m)	120.83	Passing Marks: 67
Mains Subjects	**Marks secured**	
Essay (250m)	129	Passing Marks: 25
GSM1 (250m)	98	Passing Marks: 25
GSM2 (250m)	113	Passing Marks: 25
GSM3 (250m)	104	Passing Marks: 25
GSM4 (250m)	93	Passing Marks: 25
Optional Paper-1 (250m)	136	Passing Marks: 25
Optional Paper-2 (250m)	140	Passing Marks: 25
Written Total (1750m)	813	Cutoff: 520-774
Interview (275m)	190	N/A
Final (2025m)	1003	Cutoff: 754-982

I would like to share some tips:

- ❖ Define your working hours and study hours strictly.
- ❖ Don't study while you work and don't work while you study
- ❖ Don't have this thought in your mind that clearing CSE is more important. Your work is important too. I have seen people with this attitude, "Ek Baar UPSC clear hone do, apna resignation company ke muh pe maar ke aaunga" Please don't have this attitude. Whatever you are doing, whether your business or Job, it is feeding you and taking care of your expenses. It is also helping you prepare for your bigger dream. So, respect that and finish it with grace once you clear CSE.

❑❑

22

Name: Hanul Choudhary
Rank: 191

"The UPSC process is a very lengthy process and it is very natural that there will be many up and downs in the process. What we can do to overcome is to realize that these things are natural and do not push ourselves into the negative atmosphere.

HANUL CHOUDHARY

OPTIONAL SUBJECT
Chemistry

MEDIUM
English

NATIVE PLACE
Shahpura – Jaipur (Rajasthan)

EDUCATIONAL QUALIFICATION
B.Tech – IIT Delhi (2016)

PARENTS' OCCUPATION
- **Father:** Government Teacher
- **Mother:** Homemaker

COACHING TAKEN
- GS – Vajiram
- Chemistry – DIAS

MARKS
Prelims: Paper –1: 114 and **Paper – 2:** 122

MAINS MARKS AND PERSONALITY TEST
Essay (Paper I): 122
General Studies- I (Paper II): 100
General Studies- II (Paper III):093
General Studies- III (Paper IV): 107
General Studies- IV (Paper V): 105
Optional - I (Chemistry) (Paper VI):163
Optional - II (Chemistry) (Paper VII): 159
Written Total: 849
Personality Test: 154
Final Total: 1003

MY JOURNEY

The UPSC process is a very lengthy process and it is very natural that there will be many up and downs in the process. What we can do to overcome is to realize that these things are natural and do not push ourselves into the negative atmosphere. In my upsc journey there were different ups/down and I tried to deal with them in different ways.

Preliminary failure: I could not clear the preliminary stage in my first attempt. It was a big let down as you have to wait for one more year just to have another crack at the exam. In this period, try to be in company of friends and family. They will act as pillar of support. My friends used to give me examples of many candidates who failed prelims in their first attempt but cleared all the stages in the next step. It was this support only that helped me to get back on the preparation course. I will suggest that we should take a short break before starting again with the preparation.

Crisis of options: Many people who prepare for UPSC leave very good jobs. So many times the backup option is available in case UPSC does not work. But most of the time the availability of this option becomes a major factor for the ups and down in the preparation. The idea of this availability of option often aggravates these up-downs. In these moments, we should focus on the reason why we chose this path. Focus on the struggles that you have endured during the preparation. In my case, I would always take inspiration from my school days. During 9th class, I changed my medium from Hindi to English. I changed school and moved from a government school in my hometown to an English medium school in Jaipur. I still remember the extra effort I had to put in due to the change in medium. I took inspiration from the mental strength of that 9th class kid. How that 9th class kid understood that he had to put more effort than anyone else. How he knew that he has to sacrifice on many things that his classmates do. How that kid had the mental strength to stay away from his home and to walk regularly in the afternoon sun to take tuitions. I did not want to betray the effort of that kid by giving up on the dream that he saw. This kept me motivated throughout the journey.

LIST OF BOOKS

- The basic list of books is same for each aspirant. Such list can be found in many other strategies. I will try to add some material/books which I think are less known but very beneficial.

- *Art and Culture:* Nitin Sangwan Sir's Art and Culture PDF (shared by sir on his blog)
- *GS -2 ARC summary:* D Amarkesh sir's ARC summary are very concise and informative. (Available on web)
- *GS -2 Polity section:* M Puri sir's notes
- *GS -3 Agriculture section:* Mrunal sir's website articles (even for other topics these are good)

MESSAGE FOR NEW COMERS

One thing I think we should understand before starting our preparation is that syllabus and areas UPSC exam covers is very vast. There will be areas where we will be weak and other areas were we will be more comfortable. What we should is to sharpen our comfortable areas and try to be among the best scorer in those areas. On the other hand look for ways in which you can score better in your weak areas. In my case, my optional was my strength and essay and ethics paper were my weak points. I focused on my optional to great detail. I covered chemistry from multiple books, made my own notes and tried to cover the hard topics. Here with the level of preparation I had, I was confident that I will be able to attempt more than 90% of the paper. For Ethics and Essay I focused on what were my weaknesses. I watched many videos, to get inspired from the toppers, read many strategies and tried to find out that how can I overcome my weak points and score average marks. So for these weak points, always try to find out the ways how you can score at least average marks. For essay, I mugged up different introductions on different topics to make a good first impression. For Ethics, when I went through one of the topper's copy I found that I can use the point format in the ethics paper too. As I am not a good writer these innovative methods helped me overcome this weakness. So one need to find these innovative strategies for their weaknessess.

Try to take only those things from people's strategy that you think will work for you. Everyone has different approach for this exam. Don't follow anyone's strategy blindly, try to find out which aspect of a particular strategy will work better for you.

For mains, the best piece of advice I could get was to prepare 3/4 pages of content on each and every topic in the 3 GS papers. It helped me immensely as after I cleared prelims, I had the content ready for mains. The consolidation of the different sources will take time but it will save very much precious time during prelims and mains. So be prepared with this before prelims.

❑❑

23

Name: Maninder Singh
Rank: 195

Have absolute faith in yourself, your capabilities and your hard work. Your efforts will never go unrewarded.

MANINDER SINGH

OPTIONAL SUBJECT
Geography

MEDIUM
English

NATIVE PLACE
Ambala City

PLACE OF RESIDENCE
Mohali (Punjab)

EDUCATIONAL QUALIFICATIONS
- 10th from St. Xavier's Mohali – 92%
- 12th from Shishu Niketan Chandigarh – 86%
- B. Tech. in Mechanical Engineering from IIT Jodhpur – 6.75 CGPA

PARENTS' OCCUPATION
- **Father:** Sub- Divisional Officer – Water resources department, Punjab
- **Mother:** Homemaker

COACHING DETAILS
GS from Vajiram and Ravi, Geography from Shabbir Sir (Vajiram and Ravi), test series and mock interviews given at various institutes in Chandigarh and Delhi. I want to emphasise that coaching is no substitute for hard work. In fact, you can very well clear the exam with flying colours without coaching.

MY JOURNEY

Back in June 2018, My intention behind this write-up is simple – provide a glimmer of hope. I needed a lot of motivation and read a lot of stories of successful candidates which gave me hope.

It was in May 2015 that I arrived in Delhi, started preparation, gave prelims without preparation just to get the feel of the exam and didn't clear it. I gave Punjab PCS prelims and wrote mains but couldn't clear that. I learned a very important lesson then when I switched off my phone for a while after the result.

I was still in Delhi for CSE 2016, increasingly frustrated at the rising cost of living, became an insomniac, wasn't able to sleep properly due to the noise (horns and dog barks) and started losing focus and also my mind, remaining irritated for most part of the day. I gave the interview that year and was waiting for the result on 31/5/2017 and at 7 got a big shock when I didn't see my name up on the list. But then the important lesson had been learnt: To show up a brave face especially in front of your parents because for them the result doesn't matter but your happiness and state of mind does. And they get anxious if you're not okay, especially if you're away from home. And so I acknowledged the fact that I'd indeed made very far in the first serious attempt (was extremely fortunate to get 787 in Mains- the cut-off marks for that year!).

But the expenses were taking a toll and my educational background suddenly started haunting me as I started getting swayed by societal expectations of an IITian- earning crazy money! So I decided to head back home for CSE 2017. I cleared prelims, was very happy with my attempt and was waiting for the result to be declared on 27th April. Anxiety had already started building up close to the result days. That very same time at about 7 PM came the results. I searched but didn't find my name. The important lesson came into play. Feeling devastated and numb inside, I had to pretend that everything is okay. Came back home, showed an extremely brave face to my parents, even comforted them that it doesn't matter. I blamed an easy scapegoat for the bad result- my optional subject Geography.

But an even more devastating shock awaited me on 11/5/2018 when the marks were received. I'd scored 851 in Mains (806 being the cut-off) and only 132 in the PT and missed the list by 23 marks.

CS Mains Mark sheet, 2017

Essay (Paper I): 132

General Studies- I (Paper II): 107

General Studies- II (Paper III): 114

General Studies- III (Paper IV): 125

General Studies- IV (Paper V): 095

Optional - I (Geography) (Paper VI): 125

Optional - II (Geography) (Paper VII): 153

Written Total: 851

Personality Test: 132

Final Total: 983 (Remarks: Not Recommended)

My normal thinking said that geography ruined my attempt. But PT marks were incomprehensible! Who else do I blame now? It was me myself, who did something horribly wrong at the PT and got such a low score. Yes I know PT is unpredictable, but a very low score makes you doubt yourself. I was not just blaming myself, but questioning my basic character-traits, every judgement, and every single act done in the past. It was like losing an identity, starting to hate oneself as an individual – and all due to just 30 minutes of PT.

And things only turned for the worst on 3/6/2018 – prelims for CSE 2018. I checked the answer key, was getting 94 and almost lost all hope. I hadn't slept all night. At about 6 in the morning I filled up the form for SSC, 4/6 being last date of registration. I didn't sign up for any test series, was doing nothing but staying in front of the books and engaging in destructive thought patterns. The basic thought I believe is this- 2 years of my life lost! one to wait for next prelims another one for the whole cycle to complete, apart from the other thought that 30 minutes cost me an year earlier. Regrets, what-ifs, tears, sadness, cursing luck and everything happened. And the saddest thing was thinking about my parents who I knew were getting bombarded with difficult questions about my future and yet having faith in me. This thought would make me feel like the weakest person alive. I'm pretty sure, I was on the brink. These, anyone would concur, are the early signs of depression.

However, one thought made me feel good – 'This too shall pass'. It somehow did on 14/7/2018. Prelims result came and it was such a relief that

I almost collapsed in my mother's arms while telling her the result! I knew that this is something unusual, a heavenly gift and an opportunity of a lifetime. I also discovered a new WHY: this time I was going to do it for my parents, to make them happy and proud. I prepared a schedule, got down to study and took active steps to take care of my mind and body- daily exercising and practising meditation. I was determined to give it my best try. I just wanted to be proud of my efforts in this attempt. I said to myself that whatever happens now would not be due to lack of efforts but fate. I went to a psychologist to understand what happens to me on the day of the interview to overcome that obstacle as well. And I kept saying to myself that even if I don't qualify in CSE, I've learnt to work hard and wherever else I go, I would do good enough.

As fate would have it, things changed for good on 5/4/2019. The feeling was more of a relief. I could finally see the proud faces of my parents. They'd suffered much more than I had and thoroughly deserve to be blissfully happy.

Looking back, everything about the journey makes absolute sense.A lot of lessons needed to be learnt, a lot of mistakes were to be made, a lot of strength and resilience needed to be developed, a lot of faith needed to be placed on oneself and God. There are many folks out there who didn't make it to the list. I'm sure many of them are much more capable and deserving than I am. This is where fate comes in. I was even more humbled and thankful to God for this blessing seeing my prelims score:

Prelims Score: 2018

Paper-1: 98.00 (Cut off Marks 98.00 for General.)

Paper-2: 132.50

CS Mains Mark sheet, 2018:

Essay (Paper I): 129

General Studies- I (Paper II): 110

General Studies- II (Paper III): 109

General Studies- III (Paper IV): 103

General Studies- IV (Paper V): 113

Optional - I (Geography) (Paper VI): 144

Optional - II (Geography) (Paper VII): 129

Written Total: 837

Personality Test: 165

Final Total: 1002

This journey is much more about becoming a civil servant. I am extremely fortunate to have absolute gems of persons surrounding me throughout the journey, especially my parents. I approached the UPSC journey in a positive stride- to develop such qualities that an ideal officer needs to have, to introspect deep into my personality and hone myself as a good citizen and a better person, and above all to develop an inquisitive attitude for living a lifetime of fulfilment. It is a transformational journey and my sincere advice is to approach it on these very lines. Take care of your mental and physical health and have a positive approach towards life. This exam is neither a medal of success nor a certificate of failure. It is just the means to a good career, which can be pursued in many other different ways. What ultimately would matter would be how you are as a person and how beautifully you've pursued life.

I wish every one of you the very best of luck for a great life ahead.

SUGGESTIONS FOR NEW ASPIRANTS

- Have a positive and determined approach towards the exam if you've just started preparing – no distractions, no 2nd thoughts about any back-up or anything. Just focus single-mindedly on what is in your hand – studying hard.
- Have absolute faith in yourself, your capabilities and your hard work. Your efforts will never go unrewarded. As I mentioned earlier, even if God-forbid you are unable to make it, you'll become an altogether different personality in the end and do extremely well in life.
- The market is flooded with all types of content. My sincere advice is to focus on limited content and do repeated revisions of the same material, especially for the static portions.
- This exam is not only testing the depth of your knowledge but also the breadth of your knowledge. This means that you have to work very smartly to neither have too shallow knowledge of any topic, nor too deep because you get just 200 words to express.
- As a corollary to previous point, the exam requires you to write brilliant answers that stand out from the rest, and this requires a lot of practice.

You can go through toppers' answer sheets, have a look at how they write, what structure they follow. Then try to incorporate these in your daily answer writing practice. This is one portion which is extremely important, yet is overlooked by majority of the candidates.

❖ Memorise the Mains syllabus. If not, at least put up the syllabus in front of your study table. Also go through previous years' papers. This way you'll know about the topic you're reading from any book or the newspaper and better judge its importance.

Booklist that I followed:

History: Ancient – R S Sharma Old NCERT

Medieval – NCERT Class 7

Modern – Spectrum for Prelims, Bipin Chandra for Mains

World history – Arjun Dev Old NCERTs Classes 9th and 10th (only topics mentioned in the syllabus)

Post-independence – Vision IAS summary available in ORN(Old Rajendra Nagar) + Pradhan Mantri series on Youtube

Culture – Nitin Singhania + Class 11th Fine Arts NCERT

Geography: GC Leong Environment by Shankar IAS

Society:

NCERTs for classes 11th and 12th

Polity: M. Laxmikant GS 2 notes by M. Puri Sir – available in ORN shops International relations notes by Chokhalingam Sir – available in ORN shops Governance notes by Ram Babu Sir – available in ORN shops GS3 security portion – Challenges to internal Security of India (TMH publication).

Economy portion + agriculture portions for GS3 – book by Ramesh Singh or Sriram IAS economy handout available at ORN shops

GS 4 – Lexicon

In case of any queries, suggestions or any sort of help, you can reach me at the following:

Instagram – maninder.011

❑❑

24

Name: Akshay Kabra
Rank: 207, UPSC CSE 2018
Service Allocated IRS (IT)

'Take up one idea, Make that one idea your life, dream of it, think of it, live on that idea"
–Swami Vivekanand'

AKSHAY KABRA

OPTIONAL SUBJECT
Commerce and Accountancy

MEDIUM
English

NATIVE PLACE
Jaipur, Rajasthan

PLACE OF RESIDENCE
Mohali (Punjab)

EDUCATIONAL QUALIFICATIONS
CA CS CMA LLB MCOM UGC(NET JRF)

PARENTS' OCCUPATION
- Father: Business
- Mother:

COACHING TAKEN
- For GS from vajiram and prepared optional paper by self
- Service preference IAS-IRS(IT)-IPS

MAINS: 2017
Essay (Paper I): 121
General Studies- I (Paper II): 104
General Studies- II (Paper III): 101
General Studies- III (Paper IV): 126
General Studies- IV (Paper V): 080
Optional - I (Comm. & Accountancy) (Paper VI): 119
Optional - II (Comm. & Accountancy) (Paper VII): 148
Written Total: 799

QUALIFIED IN CS (MAIN) WRITTEN EXAMINATION

So after analysing my mistakes, it was time to work upon it. I know it is not that easy to boost yourself but keep motivating yourself.

My source of motivation is my parents and the following quote of Swami Vivekanandji:

"Take up one idea, Make that one idea your life, dream of it, think of it, live on that idea"

So I enrolled for test series for GS and rankers, classes for my optional and made myself comfortable, that I could complete my papers in desired time.

MY THIS YEAR (CSE, 2018) MARKSHEET IS

Essay (Paper I): 119
General Studies- I (Paper II): 099
General Studies- II (Paper III): 101
General Studies- III (Paper IV): 120
General Studies- IV (Paper V): 098
Optional - I (Comm. & Accountancy) (Paper VI):143
Optional - II (Comm. & Accountancy) (Paper VII): 144
Written Total: 824
Personality Test: 176
Final Total: 1000

CONTACT

Facebook: https://www.facebook.com/akshay.kabra3

MY JOURNEY

From professional qualification to world of UPSC.

3 things which I always take with me while preparing

Positivity (Most Important Attribute)

Positivity: One thing that promotes positivity is the trust. One has to trust about the material he/she is referring to, the mentors which are guiding you, the near and dear ones, who are supporting you at various stages. Yes, it's a journey and not a task of a day or two. During this journey, you require constant motivation In my case, my source of motivation had been my parents and family.

Continuity: People say that continuous and consistent efforts are must but as an aspirant, I know that there are times when you feel so low and depressed that one loses the confidence of reaching the destination. Better one should take a break and divert the negatives by taking up source hobby like, I like to cook. So, in times of depression, I cook something for the family. That makes me calm and composed and make me forget my worries. This leads to continuous efforts and I stay motivated. It helps me.

Practice: Practice is a necessary evil in cracking of this exam, whether it is prelims or mains. In prelims, one has to practice lot of MCQS and in mains, practice for answer writings. And in interviews, one has to practice by going for mocks. It makes you confident and helps you handle the situation comfortably.

As I have mentioned, earlier this was my second attempt and I missed to crack interview by meager margin.

Failure definitely gives a dent as earlier I had never faced it in my professional courses but at the same time you must move on and realise what went wrong, analysing your failure definitely helps you out.

In my case, I have not practised much in my first attempt that cost me such that I was not able to complete my papers on time and in each paper left 1 to 2 questions.

Then individually, I had to improve the performance in ethics, optional and essay.

Don't believe in stereotype statements generally heard around:

- it's tough for Commerce students to crack the UPSC civil services.
- If you are a CA, then you should go for a job that's because UPSC civil services is more or less reserved for engineers
- You have to study 14 to 15 hours a day to crack civil services
- You should completely stay away from the social media and society
- Being in general category, don't go for complaining about reservations committed to few classes of the society. Instead, aim for the seats which we can have but that is very very tough to achieve.

TIPS

- UPSC is all about general knowledge. If you don't have good GK then you cannot crack the exam it's a myth. I usually got grade 'D' in my school G.K. exam. But practice makes the man perfect.
- Be sincere in your efforts.
- Hear strategies from different people, see videos but don't follow those strategies blindly. Make your unique strategy. That will help you more to clear the exam.

- It is true that preparation enhances your knowledge and make you aware of many topics but be specific in retaining the information for scoring well. Limit your studies up to knowledge but don't go towards making thesis for a PhD.

As most of the sources of toppers are available and pretty much same I will not repeat these but a few things which helped me out in answer writing.

I read the Niti Aayog's 3 years' action agenda and simultaneously *Economic Survey* as both have quite similar chapters so it gives a consolidated overview of where we are and where we ought to be. It helped a lot in essay and GS papers too.

I subscribed for Insights online main test series, which helped me to practice. Brainstorming of different questions. At same time, suggested answers helped me out in refining my answers. I also practised daily questions of insights that provides extensive coverage of newspaper. And other sources. I also followed deep learning series of la excellence youtube channel by rambabusir which in 10 to 15 minutes not only replicate the facts of editorial but analyse the essence of it. For ethics, I practised daily the questions uploaded on *insightsias* website which helped me to improve my ethics score, from my experience of previous two attempts I can definitely say that ethics is all about practice. In my second attempt what I have changed from past is to limit my sources and read them again and after each reading, trying to consolidate it for the next reading. I also followed weekly magazine of la excellence which contains essence of past weeks editorial and other news analysis paperwise and questions to practice, I focussed less on note making from newspaper and followed it only. Also for some sections, I also refered to learning space digital website which provides good content for prelims as well as mains. I just want to mention that by following what others are will not make your answers different and unique, you must push yourself to work somewhat harder and smarter to take an edge.

I also owe my success to what I achieved from my educational background.

Being a chartered accountant job experience helped me to analyse the cost benefit analysis of my scope of study. As a CA student, what we learn is to handle different subjects at a time. Intense structure of training and exposure provided me to handle my interview more effectively. And it definitely helped me to cover my optional and same goes with my other qualifications.

FOR INTERVIEWS

Its was my first face off with the interview board and the chairman was Smitanagaraj Ma'am.

As my turn was the second last in noon session, I was waiting for my turn which was quited tedious and had almost 2 to 3 cups of coffee. After a point of time, all my anxieties ended and I was normal while giving my interview which worked positively for me. For preparatory phase, I did have an anxiety and fear of interview, which I had to break.

So I joined mock interviews and used their feedbacks to improve my skills. Mock sessions of *Sankalp, Drishtias, Raus, Chanakya, ALS, Srichaitanya* were good. But be careful, don't try to change yourself completly but change only that very aspect which needs to be. For example, I am not a good debator and have a soft spoken personality so what I need to change in me is to increase my voice, balance answers with emotional and practical solutions. And I presented what I am in front of the board and not fake a personality for the sake of the interview.

MY INTERVIEW

Although I had written my papers in English, I opted for Hindi as medium of exchange in interview.

As I was from commerce background by profession and so were my optionals, interview was more focussed to recent topics such as Demonetisation, GST, Role of auditors in fraud, What india wants. A good GDP, HDI or Happiness?

In one question related to naga issues resolution I was not able to give the answer appropriately but that is a catch. Don't lose hope and take each question as a single ball and try to fetch as many runs/marks on that very question.

Overall it's a journey where you learn so many aspects of life. I definitely enjoyed each bit of it. This level of learning which create aspects of openess inclusiveness and respect for each single creature.

I can assure you all that though tough, but once you get into this the level of scope of work you can bring change into lives of many. Will be torch bearers of antyodyaya. At last, I thank my parents, friends, mentors and well wishers who gave me strength to achieve this success.

❑❑

25

Name: Kunal Aggarwal
Rank: 211, CSE, 2018

"This exam is not just about books and replicate the information available. It is about your personality, about how you can deliver with the minimal resources available at your hand like an office would have."

KUNAL AGGARWAL

OPTIONAL SUBJECT

Political Science and International Relations

MEDIUM

English

NATIVE PLACE

Sonipat, Haryana

EDUCATIONAL QUALIFICATIONS

B.Tech – IIT Hyderabad (2013)

PARENTS' OCCUPATION

- **Father:** Accountant (Private firm)
- **Mother:** Homemaker

COACHING TAKEN

- **GS:** Not full time, Ethics Crash course from GS Score and Material from GS Score
- **Optional:** From ShubhraRanjan Mam and Piyush Chaubey Sir

MARKS

Prelims: Paper – 1:105, **Paper -2:**170

MAINS MARKS AND PERSONALITY TEST

Essay (Paper I): 128

General Studies- I (Paper II): 101

General Studies- II (Paper III): 101

General Studies- III (Paper IV): 110

General Studies- IV (Paper V): 103

Optional - I (Political Science and Int. Relations) (Paper VI):153

Optional - II (Political Science and Int. Relations) (Paper VII) : 150

Written Total: 846

Personality Test: 154

Final Total: 1000

MY JOURNEY

I started my preparation in 2016 while working at *Goldman Sachs* as a technical analyst. The journey had started way back in 2015 itself after I joined a short term public policy course from a think tank in Bengaluru and did a policy bootcamp from Vision India Foundation. I decided that I will take off from my current job and try getting into civil services. I did not want to have regrets but I had a clear timeline of maximum 3 attempts after which I will take up a job again in private sector. So, 2016 preliminary exam was in few months and I started preparing full time since April 2nd week. I had certain preconceived notions about the exam. I thought that preparing the static portion and doing a part of current affairs would be enough. At least that is what I was told based on previous years. But this couldn't work. This almost never works for UPSC and realized it right after my prelims.

So, now I had a year to prepare in detail. I started with same basic books (majorly NCERT) and attempted one test per week. I made sure that each subject to be best which can I prepare. Daily current affairs had to be done regularly. I used to follow *Civilsdaily* for my current affairs. I would rely on them at later stages for my answer writing practice as well. I joined a Mains test series (at GS Score) in December 2016 itself so that I am well prepared for Mains 2017. Answer writing practice at that time pays off even today. Now, General Studies was well in control, both static and current affairs. But I knew I had to complete my optional subject as well. I got access to Piyush Chaubey Sir's lectures videos and this helped me build a base conceptually. But that's all I did. That is probably the biggest mistake I did in my 2017 preparation.

Prelims 2017 was cleared and preparation for mains started. I joined Chaubey sir's crash course for PSIR. That helped but only to a limited extent because I had not really prepared the subject before prelims. Fortunately, I had GS well prepared. So, I could spend more time on optional. Luckily, I cleared through Mains as well but the next stage was again a task at hand. I was an under confident person while talking to such senior people (I would still be hesitant at times) but that took me down. I missed the final list by 26 marks.

Now, the journey to a big attempt (my third attempt) started. During this attempt, I had talked to my father that I would take a job if I do not clear prelims. He was a bit worried. So, I assured him and prepared for prelims. The stages kept on going till personality test round. This time, I joined Shubhra

Ma'am as I knew her material for PSIR is best and she provides all the scholars, theories needed for exam. I would need to understand them and use them while crafting my answer. So, I just followed what she said. This paid off. I had less marks in Essay as well in 2017. So, I knew I had to increase marks there. I joined a test series but I collected more content specifically for essay. From what I understand even today, I needed to have some catchy phrases, needed to design my essays better and connect them with real world examples more. So, I did it and improved. The efforts paid off with improved marks in both optional and essay. I finally secured rank 211. I wasn't very happy initially because I wanted under 150 (IFS is my 2nd choice!). But then, I was a relief. Parents were happy and so was I.

The journey continued. I started preparing again and I am hoping to write mains. Life is journey and we always tend to find new challenges for ourselves. The journey to Rank 211 has been an experience. It was an experience full of learning, full of mood swings, testing my patience and zeal to get through.

MESSAGE FOR NEWCOMERS

Firstly, I believe that we take it too hard on ourselves to clear the exam. This exam is not just about books and replicating the information available. It is about your personality, about how you can deliver with the minimal resources available at your hand like an office would have. We should see it as a journey, only as a means to an end. This allows you to relax and concentrate better. Stakes should never be so high that you can't even study because of the tension.

Secondly, the world is full of material, books, tests and feedback. This is dangerous. One thing that I always kept in my mind was originality. One of my teachers had told me once. It is important how I think of a topic, how I analyze it and how I would write it. It is tempting to try out new material but it is not needed. We must make sure that we restrict ourselves to the resources and keep revising them.

Thirdly, syllabus is never complete and you are never 100% prepared. So, don't try to achieve that stage. We must practice with little knowledge we have. Objective questions as well as answer writing are an important part of the process. Beyond knowledge, it requires technique and strategy to attend prelims' questions. For Mains answer writing, it is an art, an art which requires structuring and crafting of your knowledge.

Fourthly, note making is of utmost important. They need to be limited too. You need to be able to revise them. Prelims notes should be readable in 3-4 days and Mains notes should be readable in 10-12 days at the maximum. So, choose what you write in your notes. I used to question myself along the lines, is it important for the country, is it something that I could forget and would need to revisit.

❑❑

26

Name: Pankaj Lamba
Rank: 236, CSE-2018

"It is very important to remain positive and train your brain not to go into negativity. If one can control his emotions and maintain his composure throughout the process, he will surely succeed."

PANKAJ LAMBA

OPTIONAL SUBJECT
Law

MEDIUM
English

NATIVE PLACE
VPO Dalanwas, Distt Mahendergarh, Haryana

EDUCATIONAL QUALIFICATIONS
- MSc (Hons) Economics—BITS Pilani'17
- BE (Hons) Civil---BITS Pilani'17

PARENTS' OCCUPATION
- **Father:** Inspector RPF, Faridabad
- **Mother:** Homemaker

COACHING TAKEN
- **GS:** Self study
- **Law:** Nirvana

MARKS
Prelims: Paper – 1: 116.66 and **Paper -2:** 130.83

MAINS MARKS AND PERSONALITY TEST
Essay (Paper I): 113
General Studies- I (Paper II): 085
General Studies- II (Paper III): 117
General Studies- III (Paper IV): 100
General Studies- IV (Paper V): 109
Optional - I (Law) (Paper VI):142
Optional - II (Law) (Paper VII): 155
Written Total: 821
Personality Test: 176
Final Total: 997

MY JOURNEY

The journey of UPSC has lots of ups and downs. The sheer number of candidates and increasing competition always makes one anxious whether he/she can do it or not. I firmly believe that having good support in form of friends, family and teachers can help you in charting out the journey of UPSC.

My law teacher once said 'UPSC preparation is 90% mental training and the rest is curricular training.' Different people have different capacities. They have different strengths and weaknesses. Hence it is very important to remain positive and train your brain not to go into negativity. If one can control his emotions and maintain his composure throughout the process, he will surely succeed.

Last year I was not able to clear mains. But one good thing was that I knew that it was not my best performance and there were lot of areas of improvement. So I took the failure as a chance to improve myself and come back strongly.

Having a close group of motivating friends and talking to my parents helped me in managing stress during the examination process, which is rather a lengthy assignment. They helped me to stay strong and kept my confidence high.

During my school days, I wanted to join IIT. I went to Kota for coaching as well, but things couldn't materialize. Failure of not getting admission in IIT made me feel really sad. In those days my father once said to me, "Do you think every successful person in India is an IITian? Success in life depends not on the college tag but one's zeal to conquer and keep moving even when the chips are down". He was right! We need to move forward and look for better opportunities that is on our way.

MESSAGE TO NEW COMERS

Swami Vivekananda once said,"कोई लक्ष्य मनुष्य के साहस से बड़ा नहीं, हारा वही है जो लड़ा नहीं |"

This quote has always inspired me and I hope that it inspires you as well.

I do not want to share much about how to study, what to study because there are plenty of sources, books and other materials already available in market/internet. It will just be a repeat of the same things. However I would like to say that please be positive and don't lose hope.I had been a very ordinary student. I somehow managed to pass my engineering that too with a very average score. I can say with conviction that if I can do it, you can also do it. Just believe in yourself and do smart study. Do not fall in the trap of market which is filled with bulky books, photocopied reading materials etc. Rather focus on concise notes and understanding core issues and demand of question.

This exam according to me is more about one's character and the ability to stay and rise back even after failures. Therefore, strong will power or grit is a key requirement.

Additionally, I would also like to say that one must enjoy the journey of UPSC. My law teacher says "You'll be IAS only when you enjoy the path to IAS. Sad people don't clear this exam". It is truth. We have to see UPSC journey as a learning experience, then only we can succeed. A person who is considering preparation as a burden is not on right track I believe.

I would also like to share few lines with you, which I read recently--

You do not have to come first in the race,

You do not need to leave everyone behind!

It is important to join your race,

It is important that you fall and stand again!

There will be many tests in life,

Those who are ahead today will follow you tomorrow!

Just you don't leave,

Just don't give up fighting!

Lastly, I want to share two quotes, which are close to me: "Hope is a good thing, may be the best thing, and no good thing ever dies"

– Shawshank Redemption.

"Success is not final, failure is not fatal, it is the courage to continue is what matters".

– Winston Churchill.

Best of luck! Hope you all succeed in your endeavours.

❑❑

27

Name: Manjeet Singh
Rank: 256, CSE-2018

"Our greatest glory is not in never falling, but in rising every time we fall."

MANJEET SINGH

OPTIONAL SUBJECT
PS & IR

MEDIUM
English

NATIVE PLACE
Village Ladwa, Dist. Hisar, Haryana

EDUCATIONAL QUALIFICATIONS
Graduation through Correspondence from Delhi University in English Literature

PARENTS' OCCUPATION
- Mother: Homemaker

COACHING TAKEN OR SELF STUDY
Coaching taken for Optional

MY JOURNEY

(a) **Struggle part:** I got selected in my last (6th) attempt. I gave my first attempt in 2013, cleared Prelims but did not write Mains as I was not prepared. In 2014, again cleared Pre and wrote Mains but could not qualify the same. Then for 2 consecutive years (2015 & 2016), I could not qualify even the Prelims; once failing by 1 mark and next time by 10 marks. In 2017, I reached till interview but failed to make it to the list. And finally I was able to get a rank in 2018.

(b) **Study plan/list of books:** Main focus was on NCERT and standard reference books like Laxmikanth for Polity, Ramesh Singh for Economics, Nitin Singhania notes for Culture, Shankar IAS for Environment, Spectrum for Indian Freedom Struggle etc. During these 6 years of preparations, I also covered some other books like *Hot, Flat and Crowded*, *"Small is Beautiful"*, *"Limits to Growth"* and *The Argumentative Indian* etc. I made short notes out of these books. These helped me with introduction and conclusion part as well as punchlines for the interview.

Marks in CSE 2018

Prelims	
Paper 1	102
Paper 2	135
Mains	
SUBJECTS	MARKS
Essay (Paper-I)	137
General Studies -I (Paper-Ii)	101
General Studies -Ii (Paper-Iii)	116
General Studies -Iii (Paper-Iv)	092
General Studies -Iv (Paper-V)	079
Optional-I (Political Science & International	
Relations) (Paper-Vi)	141
Optional-Ii (Political Science & International	
Relations) (Paper-Vii)	142
Written Total	808
Personality Test	187
Final Total	995

MESSAGE TO NEWCOMERS

Prepare for a long battle. There are candidates who clear it in first attempt. You may or may not be among them. If you are one of those brilliant stars then congratulations. But if you are not one of those who crack it in first attempt then be ready for a long drawn struggle.

Try to stick to basics like NCERT and standard reference books. There is always a book which some other aspirant has read and you have not. But it hardly matters. UPSC is not looking for Gyanis who know everything, rather, they are looking for managers those who can manage with limited resources. And as often is said, "Instead of reading 100 books once, read 10 books 10 times."

Try to minimise the distractions as much as possible. Do not get drawn in meaningless debates. They do nothing else than destroying your time and attempts.

Believe in yourself because no one in the world except you knows what you are truly capable of doing. All other people judge you by your achievements and failures. But you alone know your true potential.

Know the reason why you want to be a part of Civil Services. Because the strength of your purpose will give you strength to move on when the moving gets tough.

❑❑

28

Name: Inderveer Singh
Rank: CSE 2018 – 259; IFS 2018 – 7

"Have a clarity of thought (why Civil Services); this is because the exam is becoming very competitive day by day. One needs to have a strong source of motivation to complete the journey even if failures come in aspirant's way."

INDERVEER SINGH

OPTIONAL SUBJECT
CSE – Geography; IFS – Geology and Forestry

MEDIUM
English

NATIVE PLACE
Merta Road, Nagaur, Rajasthan

EDUCATIONAL QUALIFICATIONS
B. Tech., Mechanical Engineering, IIT Kanpur, 2015

PARENTS' OCCUPATION
- **Father:** Mining Engineer
- **Mother:** Homemaker

COACHING TAKEN OR SELF-STUDY
GS: Self-study; Geography – Neetu Singh madam

MARKS
Prelims 2018: Paper 1: 116; **Paper 2:** 128.33

MAINS MARKS AND PERSONALITY TEST
Essay (Paper I): 131
General Studies- I (Paper II): 090
General Studies- II (Paper III): 109
General Studies- III (Paper IV): 105
General Studies- IV (Paper V): 093
Optional - I (Geography) (Paper VI): 141
Optional - II (Geography) (Paper VII): 161
Written Total: 830
Personality Test: 165
Final Total: 995

MY JOURNEY

(a) **Struggle**

1. *'Seeds' for my Civil Services preparation:* During an internship after my second year of college, I got a chance to work with many IAS and IPS officers. I interacted with them very freely and they gave me a lot of insights into Civil Services. I was very impressed by the opportunities these services offer to serve public and the diverse profile of work these services have.
2. *'Starting' the preparation:* I had made my mind to join Civil Services during my final year of graduation. Since then I am fully committed to this goal and it has been almost 4 years journey. The driving force has been the interest in public service as a career option. I have tried to do public service in many ways earlier during my graduation as well viz. project on prosthetic limbs, vegetable cutting machine for visually challenged, etc. thus it was a passion for me.
3. *'Rigour' of the preparation:* In spite of strong interest in Civil Services, when failures hit on your face, one feels like quitting. Not just the mental, emotional or physical toll that this exam takes, but it also shakes your self-confidence. I kept myself moving by recalling a saying that 'anything that does not kill you makes you stronger'. I had left a well-paying job, an opportunity to go to US, just to live a life of my choice. And I am not going to quit, I will never give up. This spirit to fight for your choice has its root in my family background as we have been doing farming in Western Rajasthan where drought is the normal situation and quitting was never an option.
4. *'Support' system during preparation:* My family's trust in me has made me swim this long. They always kept me motivated and positive. Giving a positive response to any setback and openness to learn from mistakes have been some of the keys of success which my parents gave me.

(b) **List of books:** Apart from some standard books, I have been benefited from these:

1. *Art and Culture:* CCRT website
2. *Polity:* ARC notes available in market

3. *Current Affairs:* Forum IAS classes
4. *Essay:* Lukmaan IAS test series

MESSAGE FOR NEW COMERS

1. "Have a clarity of thought (why Civil Services); this is because the exam is becoming very competitive day by day. One needs to have a strong source of motivation to complete the journey even if failures come in aspirant's way."
2. Don't be in a haste: Do full research about this exam, resources required during preparation, back-up options, etc. and then jump into it. Else we end up wasting some attempts without being prepared adequately.
3. Have a support mechanism: It may be parents, siblings, friends, etc. on whom you may fall back in times of crisis and low self-confidence.

❑❑

29

Name: Anju

Rank: AIR-272 (CSE 2018), AIR- 398(CSE 2016)

"There are no shortcuts to success. If you desire for something you will surely get it provided you consistently work hard for it without wasting time."

ANJU

OPTIONAL SUBJECT
Public Administration

MEDIUM
English

NATIVE PLACE
Jind (Haryana)

EDUCATIONAL QUALIFICATIONS
BA (Maths, Economics), MBA Finance

PARENTS' OCCUPATION
- Father: Farmer
- Mother: Teacher

MARKS
CSE 2016

MAINS MARKS AND PERSONALITY TEST

MARKS: CSE 2016
- Essay: 126
- GS I: 116
- GS II: 108
- GS III: 116
- GS IV: 132
- Optional I: 136
- Optional II: 139
- Interview: 129
- Final Total: 1002

MARKS: CSE 2018
- Mains (Total – 862)
- Essay – 127
- GS I – 92
- GS II – 120
- GS III – 105
- GS IV – 85
- Optional I – 168
- Optional II – 165
- Interview – 132
- Final Total - 994

MY JOURNEY

(a) **Ups and Downs and How to deal with them:** Hello everyone! My name is Anju, my story is a bit different from the other aspirants. I am married and a mother too. I started my preparation at a very late stage. After marriage your responsibilities increase tremendously especially when you are a working mother. I always had a dream to appear for Civil Services, but somewhere I used to think it a bit impossible. I had no one to guide me, I had no one to look upon to. But I was lucky enough to get a very supportive husband and the guidance of one of my classmates, Surender Punia (APFC). When Surender started preparation and cleared prelims in the first attempt I got some confidence and got his guidance too.

I appeared for the first time in CSE 2014, I wrote Mains, but was not sure that I would clear. But I cleared, and appeared for interview, but couldn't get through that year. Next attempt i.e. CSE 2015, I couldn't clear the prelims. In CSE 2016, I had my own reference point, I knew where I had to make improvements, and worked upon it. I got rank 398 in 2016 and was allocated IRS-C&CE.

After joining the service, I realised that IRS-C&CE provides a lots of opportunities along with better work life balance. It provides the opportunity to work in Customs, GST, Narcotics; the prime institutions like DRI, DGGI,ED,CBI; Foreign Postings like with COIN,WCO,WTO etc.I again appeared for the exam though half heartedly, as I was not too keen for IAS. I got rank 272 in 2018 and I topped my optional too with 333 marks, which had been my weakest point right from my first attempt when I secured just 173 marks in the optional.

(b) **List of Books:** So I read very basic books and kept my sources very limited:

- History – Spectrum, NCERTs for Medieval and Ancient India
- Art and Culture – Nitin Singhania
- Polity – Laxmikant
- Environment – Shankar IAS book
- Geography – Class XI and XII NCERTs + G.C. Leong
- Science- Vision Current Affairs only

- Current Affairs- Daily Newspaper reading (Th Hindu, Indian Express Editorials and Explained Portion)
- Some Websites- PRS, PIB, Insights, IDSA, etc.

Message Newcomers

My message to the newcomers and the current aspirants is very simple – have faith in yourself and your capabilities.There are no shortcuts to success. If you desire for something, you will surely get it, provided you work for it without wasting time. You best know yourself, the strategy that may work for one person may not work for the other. So listen to others' advice but choose selectively. I have seen many capable persons not getting through just because of succumbing to wrong advice and pressure. Keep your reading material limited and revise it time and again.

❑❑

30

Name: Anshul Jain
Rank: 285, CSE-2018

"Self-discipline, self-belief and being brutally honest to oneself are the basic necessities to clear civil services exam."

ANSHUL JAIN

OPTIONAL SUBJECT
Anthropology

MEDIUM
English

NATIVE PLACE
Ganaur, Sonepat, Haryana

EDUCATIONAL QUALIFICATION
❖ B.Tech (Civil Engineering) – IIT (BHU) Varanasi, 2016

PARENTS' OCCUPATION
❖ **Father:** Businessman
❖ **Mother:** Homemaker

COACHING TAKEN
❖ GS – Vajiram and Ravi, Delhi
❖ Anthropology – Vaid's ICS, Delhi

MARKS
Prelims: Paper -1: 126.66 and **Paper -2:** 167.50

MAINS MARKS AND PERSONALITY TEST
Essay (Paper I): 142
General Studies- I (Paper II): 85
General Studies- II (Paper III): 112
General Studies- III (Paper IV): 99
General Studies- IV (Paper V): 108
Optional - I (Anthropology) (Paper VI)-150
Optional - II (Anthropology) (Paper VII)- 157
Written Total- 853 **Personality Test-** 140 ❖ **Final Total:** 993

CONTACT
Blog: https://medium.com/@anshjain1223

MY JOURNEY

- I had many fascinations about what I would do in life when I grow up and Civil Serviceswas never one of them. In fact, I never had a clear idea about my career even after graduating from IIT (BHU) in 2016. It took three months of self-analysis and very strong persuasion by my father for me to decide that I will appear for this exam.
- When I started my preparation, I had lot of fears and doubts about my capabilities. But I narrowed down my thoughts on hard work, just sincere and dedicated hard work. I started my preparation in September 2016 and till March 2017, I was not sure whether I should appear in prelims or not as I was not very confident about my Mains preparation. At last, I decided to appear and cleared Prelims 2017. But my fears became reality as I could not clear the Mains exam that year.
- This failure made me to resolve that I won't leave any stone unturned in the next attempt. This time I focused on completing the syllabus as exhaustively as possible and practiced for mains on daily basis. My hard work paid off and I got a call for personality test.
- I had the interview on Day 1 and this made me more nervous and anxious. What will be asked by the Board? This was the constant question in my mind which I could not answer till the hour of interview. However, I kept on telling myself that not everyone who prepare for this exam get the opportunity to face the interview Board. And since I have this privilege, I must relish this experience and try to make the most of this opportunity. I have to just give my best answer at that moment and it will be a win. Overall, I felt that the interview went well but as you can see in the mark sheet the interview Board had the contrary view. This is very common in UPSC preparation, you might not get what you expect but you shall accept it, learn from it and move ahead.
- There is a peculiar thing about UPSC that when the results are expected to be declared, there is lot of hue and cry among the aspirants. The anxiety and nervousness was at peak. The feelings of the moment when you search and find your name in the list can't be explained in words. But the maximum pleasure and satisfaction comes from the contentment you see on the face of your parents.
- For me, UPSC journey has been all about learning. Learning about the world, the nation and most importantly about myself. It has been a roller

coaster ride full of lows and highs but what kept me going is my belief in hardwork. As they say, the end of one journey marks the beginning of a new one.

Message for Newcomers

- I think self-discipline, self-belief and being brutally honest to oneself are the basic necessities to clear civil services exam. Surround yourself with positive people and stay focused towards the goal.
- The most important thing that I learnt during this journey is how to tackle failure. Every aspirant faces a phase when (s)he has a self-doubt. But what matters is how quickly you overcome it and maintain consistency in your preparation. I believe that anyone and everyone can clear this exam if he/she works hard in the right direction. Just keep moving ahead and one day you will reach the destination. You will lose only when you stop trying.
- Also, there is no shortcut to the success. You'll have to work hard day in and out, leave the rest to your destiny. The journey of UPSC preparation is full of learning and at the end of day; you should strive to become a better citizen, a better human being.

❑❑

31

Name: Vasudha Sehrawat
Rank: 310, CSE-2018

"This exam is all about dedication, hard work and smartness. Try to learn from your mistakes and overcome your shortcomings."

VASUDHA SEHRAWAT

OPTIONAL SUBJECT
Geography

MEDIUM
English

NATIVE PLACE
Village Rangpuri, New Delhi

EDUCATIONAL QUALIFICATION

- Class 12th - Ryan InternationalSchool, Vasant Kunj, Delhi (Subject- PCM+ Economics) B.E -Delhi College of Engineering(Subject- Civil Engineering)

PARENTS' OCCUPATION

- **Father:** Government Service (DeputySecretary in GNCT of Delhi)
- **Mother:** Homemaker

COACHING TAKEN

- Coaching/Self Study:Both

MARKS

Prelims: Paper -1: 112.66 and **Paper -2:** 117.50

MAINS MARKS AND PERSONALITY TEST

Essay (Paper I): 132
General Studies- I (Paper II): 79
General Studies- II (Paper III): 106
General Studies- III (Paper IV): 102
General Studies- IV (Paper V): 104
Optional - I (Geography) (Paper VI)-118
Optional - II (Geography) (Paper VII)- 156
Written Total- 797 Personality Test- 193 ❖ Final Total: 990

MY JOURNEY

Struggle/Strategy: This was my 5th attempt and 4th interview. In my 4th attempt, I made it to the Reserve List of CSE-2016 (Rank 35 in RL) and was allocated AFHQ CS. The journey thus far has been very challenging. I faced repeated failures in my first three attempts, despite reaching the interview stage. However, support from my family and my determination and hard work finally paid off. While preparing for the exam, I tried to follow an integrated approach for Prelims and Mains, preparing both simultaneously. For General Studies, my focus was on revising the static portion again and again and updating the recent developments from newspapers and magazines. The source for General Studies was my notes for all subjects + Lakshmikanth (Polity) + Science Reporter (S&T) + NCERT(History) + Economic Survey, IYB, NCERT(Economics). Current Affairs part related to GS was updated from The Hindu, Yojna and Kurukshetra. For Geography, both GS and Optional, I studied my notes and certain books like Savindra Singh's Physical Geography (Paper-2), Savindra Singh's Geomorphology, Savindra Singh's Climatology, Majid Hussain's Geographical Thought (Paper-1). For Essay, which plays a very important role in one's selection, I did regular practice of essay writing.

Message to Newcomers: Don't let the failures overpower your goal. This exam is all about dedication, hard work and smartness. Try to learn from your mistakes and overcome your shortcomings. This way, nobody can stop you from achieving your dreams.

❑❑

32

Name: Aditya Kumar Jha
Rank: 339, CSE-2018

The Civil Services Examination is a journey, not an examination. In this, intelligence, hard work and long commitment is mandatory. Available study materials, resources, patient management of time can make the path of success easier.

ADITYA KUMAR JHA

OPTIONAL SUBJECT
Sanskrit Lit.

MEDIUM
English

NATIVE PLACE
Lakhnor, Madhubani (Bihar)

EDUCATION QUALIFICATION
❖ M.A. Allahabad University

PARENTS' OCCUPATION
❖ **Father:** Professor
❖ **Mother:** Housewife

MARKS
Prelims: 102

MAINS MARKS AND PERSONALITY TEST
CSE, 2016
841 + 154
CSE, 2017
830 + 184
CSE, 2018
820 + 168

Children of rural middle-class families of India as soon as they hear and think the of the term 'civil service career', their eyes sparkle with a thrill. In a village in the remote Madhubani district of Bihar was a child boy, overwhelmed by the same wonderful dreams of civil service and thrill of fame. My father is a Sanskrit professor. Till now all Sanskrit scholars have been teachers in the house. My father had a desire to become somewhat special for our 3 brothers. As a result of this in class 6 I was sent to Allahabad with my elder brother. Reaching Allahabad, made it seem closer to the dream of civil service. The childhood seed of the form came into contact with the fertile soil of Allahabad and took the form of the plant. My disciplinary elders were preparing themselves for UPSC, so this this dedication and devotion was cultivated in me since the very beginning.

Well now I have reached Intermediate (after few years). Like all children, before me, the question was what will be the next step? The conscience gave a unilateral decision as if the civil service. Then we also took admission in Allahabad University which was popularly known as IAS factory. Now the question was about the topics for the optional subjects? Subjects running the race to dozens of locally selected candidates; selected Geography, Sanskrit, and Political Science as BA subjects. With the same logic same Sulabh Budhjit said that we will pass prelims on the power of geography with a pinch and Sanskrit in Mains, the availability of tremendous numbers in geography will be ensured. Well because of this enthusiasm during B.A. there could be concrete command on the optional subject.

After doing MA in 2012, I had come to Delhi now. I was in awe of CSAT at that time. There was panic. According to the ritual, we also went to Delhi for coaching. Due to poor quality and low level coaching the preparation could not be done according to the high standards required for clearing UPSC. Meanwhile, in 2013, a change in curriculum changed strategy, breaking my confidence. For these reasons, not taking the 2013 exam, for an alternative career turned to the state civil service. Meanwhile, at first I got selected in IB as Assistant Central Intelligence Officer.

After talking to senior officials, it was decided not to join IB. On this matter my dad was very upset. I played this gamble between his insecurity causing much heartburn.

My fear of CSAT and negligible results in Hindi medium both broke my confidence. But I came up with new and amazing energy in 2015. I achieved 13th rank in Hindi medium this year, CSAT.

The success of the movement gave new energies to millions of candidates like me.

The first attempt in the Civil Services Examination, 2015. I appeared in the mains examination with full energy and enthusiasm. A circle of many hardworking friends including Ajitesh, Deepak and Dhirendra had also been formed in this onerous journey working towards our dream. Also district savings in UPPCS I got the second success as an officer.

In the Mains exam, the inborn curse of Hindi medium education, poor coaching, lack of study material, result of main examination due to self carelessness, superstition, habit of not making notes remained negative.

After missing the 2015 main examination, I took the 2016 exam with re-doubled enthusiasm. Still optional subject had become a solid hold on Sanskrit. The test series, general studies also outperformed the average. After satisfactory performance in the main examination, joining the district savings officer in Etah district as new On February 21, 2017, the main examination was successful and shared this good news with everyone, including my family. Then at about 9 o'clock in the same night, a fatal accident caused a foot fracture. I reached the hospital soon. Then for the next two months there was a wonderful preparation for the interview while being bed-ridden. Mock interview for Mukherjee Nagar with Rajendra Nagar on the wheelchair. Then on 21 April, Saxena attended the interview on Sir's board in a wheel chair. Interview was average and there was no hope of success.

On May 31 2017, as soon as I saw my name at 503th place at 7 pm, I suddenly felt confident. The tears in life did not fail due to dozens of exams, it suddenly succeeded in the second attempt. Could not stop myself after all now my life was completely changed. My dad's life the greatest spiritual practice was seen to be complete to an extent.

Keeping this enthusiasm constant, I gave the main examination of Civil Survey Examination 2017 and training of IRAS. I Joined DANICS service and obtained 431th rank in the 2017 Civil Services Examination. Now I got a boost in my enthusiasm. Then the result of the 2018 civil services examination came in April 2019.The result was shocking overall for Hindi medium. Only 2 results came out in the general category through Hindi medium. One mine and one more of the candidate. I had to be satisfied with partial success as a 339 rank. Still satisfied that this was also success in the terrible storm. Success with the blessing of God, gurus, family and friends. There have been many opportunities to climb the steps. I am currently serving as a DANICS service trainee. Every day, on the principle of 'Charaiveti', I am trying to progress continuously after learning something new from each asset.

❑❑❑

33

Name: Prateek Bayal
Rank: 340, CSE-2018

"Set your goal right. Your decision to join Civil Services should have strong foundation and correct motivation."

PRATEEK BAYAL

OPTIONAL SUBJECT
Physics

MEDIUM
English

NATIVE PLACE
Delhi

EDUCATIONAL QUALIFICATION
❖ B.Tech – IIT Delhi (2014)

PARENTS' OCCUPATION
❖ **Father:** Retired Central Government Employee
❖ **Mother:** Aanganwadi Worker

COACHING TAKEN
❖ GS – Vajiram
❖ Physics – DIAS

MARKS
Prelims: Paper -1: 122 and Paper -2: 105

MAINS MARKS AND PERSONALITY TEST
Essay (Paper I): 139
General Studies- I (Paper II): 80
General Studies- II (Paper III): 98
General Studies- III (Paper IV): 87
General Studies- IV (Paper V): 86
Optional - I (Physics) (Paper VI) -166
Optional - II (Physics) (Paper VII) - 156
Written Total- 812 Personality Test- 176 ❖ Final Total: 988

MY JOURNEY

(a) How to overcome the ups/down-

- Just remember why you started at the first place.
- Remain in a good company of like minded people/aspirants (if you can). Stay away from negative people.
- Always remember that it is natural to have some anxiety, "A ROCKET flies when its tail is on FIRE". Try to learn living with that as normal.
- Maintain good health; Do regular Exercises/Yoga/Meditation, whatever suits you.
- Never fall into any argument with anyone. Stay humble and always try to listen more than speaking. Respect views of others as well as remain FIRM yet POLITE.
- Understand the examination pattern, its demand and cost benefit analysis of various sections of examination. Though it is suggested not to leave any part of the syllabus but every individual needs to set his/her priorities as per his/her level of expertise in each paper/section.
- Do not waste time in non- productive activities; do not procrastinate.
- Watch Success Stories, Strategies and Topper's Talk for selected candidates and devise your own strategy. It will also give you motivation as well as one can identify similar struggle of selected candidates when they were preparing.
- Give equal importance to reading, studying, writing and revision.

  Revise!! Revise!! Revise!!

(b) List of Books:

- Follow Vision IAS test series module. They have listed the Primary and Secondary sources. Follow them syllabus wise along with own wisdom considering above points in mind.

Message for newcomers

- Set your goal right. Your decision to join Civil Services should have strong foundation and correct motivation. Ask Yourself, Why do you want to join Civil Services? ; Jot down the points that come to your mind and whenever you feel low keep on revisiting these points.

- Go through the exam pattern, syllabus and stages and complete process. Please be clear that all the stages of the Civil Services Examination (Prelims, Mains & Interview) have to be cleared all at once. So be clear that it is utmost important to keep patience and maintain motivation and efficiency throughtout the examination process until your final selection with desired service.
- In this era of information, there is a huge information asymmetry. In the ocean of information, rather than knowing what to study, it is more important to know what not to study and prioritize accordingly.
- Remember General Studies is a Generalist exam only and doesn't require much deep knowledge while optional subjects require personal interest, aptitude as well as adequate expertise. Thus do not worry much for General studies and do exercise prudence while choosing optional paper.

34

Name: Natisha Mathur
Rank: 351, CSE-2018

"A positive attitude, self confidence, family support, hard work and a lot of revision - these are the essential things for clearing civil services exam."

NATISHA MATHUR

OPTIONAL SUBJECT
Political Science and International Relations

MEDIUM
English

NATIVE PLACE
Delhi (Village Mohammadpur Majri)

EDUCATIONAL QUALIFICATION
❖ Graduation and Post Graduation in Political Science Hons. (Delhi University)

PARENTS' OCCUPATION
❖ **Father:** Businessman
❖ **Mother:** Housewife

COACHING TAKEN
❖ Taken in 2015-16 from Sriram's IAS after that focused on self study only.

MARKS
Prelims: GS 108 **and CSAT:** 134.18

MAINS MARKS AND PERSONALITY TEST
Essay (Paper I): 134
General Studies- I (Paper II): 102
General Studies- II (Paper III): 101
General Studies- III (Paper IV): 88
General Studies- IV (Paper V): 101
Optional - I(PS & IR) (Paper VI)-146
Optional - II (PS & IR) (Paper VII)- 149
Written Total- 821 Personality Test- 165 ❖ **Final Total:** 986

MY JOURNEY

- This was my third attempt. I could not even clear prelims in my first two attempts. The preparation from scratch every time I failed in prelims required a lot of strength. Sometimes, I used to doubt my capabilities. But because I had the support of my parents, who never let me feel down really helped me keep going in the direction of my dream of clearing UPSC. And today I am very happy that I am the first girl from my family and my village who could clear this exam.

Books List

Start from **NCERT** because they form the bedrock of this exam. Then there are some standard books like Laxmikant for polity, Shankarias for environment, Sriram's IAS notes for economics, Nitin Singhania 's book on art and culture and atlas. ARC report is important for ethics paper. One should also focus on answer writing practise. Daily newspaper reading is very important because current affairs form an important part in every stage of this exam.

- For my optional I studied from Shubhraranjan Ma'am's notes. Apart from that I went through Andrew Heywood books on political ideologies and politics, and Rajeev Bhargava and Ashok Acharya's book on political theory.
- **Message to newcomers:** a positive attitude, self confidence, family support, hard work and a lot of revision - these are the essential things for clearing this exam. In this exam, essay and ethics paper are really important. for my essay paper, I wrote about 10-15 essays on the previous years' general topics like education, technology, etc and got it checked from my brother and my friends. It is necessary to critically examine where one is lacking. That helps to improve. Also while writing the essay, I tried to cover the topic from various aspects like social, political, economic, etc. Try collecting some important quotes of Gandhiji, Dr.Abdul Kalam, etc. and use them in essay.
- For ethics paper, go through the syllabus thoroughly and write definition of each and every word written in the syllabus. Try to include examples from your life in some of the answers.
- For those who after the prelims exam get marks on the border line, please do make sure that you do not waste time in anticipation. Please utilise that one and a half month in covering your optional and essay.

- Also I want the new comers to know that this exam is very unpredictable. There is always a little bit of luck in this exam. Hence with this exam we should make sure that we side by side give other exams too. I cleared the CGL exam in 2017 and hence I was free from the fear of getting nowhere if I failed in UPSC exam. I could prepare with more focus and with free mind this time.

❑❑

35

Name: Tarun Tomar
Rank: AIR 374, CSE-2018

"If you have an aim set in your mind, work hard to achieve it. Things will occasionally go bad during the course of your journey, but there's nothing which can't be overcome by determination, grit, hard-work and perseverance."

TARUN TOMAR

OPTIONAL SUBJECT
Sociology

MEDIUM
English

NATIVE PLACE
Rohtak (Haryana)

EDUCATIONAL QUALIFICATION
❖ Bachelor in Engineering (B.E.) in Electrical and Electronics Engineering (EEE) from BITS Pilani

PARENTS' OCCUPATION
❖ **Father:** Late Shri Krishan, Earlier Principal in Haryana Govt.
❖ **Mother:** Parmeshwari Devi, Homemaker

COACHING TAKEN
❖ No

MARKS
Prelims: Paper -1: 104 and Paper -2: 161.68

MAINS MARKS AND PERSONALITY TEST
Essay (Paper I): 141
General Studies- I (Paper II): 92
General Studies- II (Paper III): 111
General Studies- III (Paper IV): 97
General Studies- IV (Paper V): 108
Optional - I(Sociology) (Paper VI)-143
Optional - II (Sociology) (Paper VII)- 130
Written Total- 822 Personality Test- 162 ❖ Final Total: 984

CONTACT
Facebook https://m.facebook.com/TarunTomer777

MY JOURNEY

I am **Tarun Tomar**. I was born and brought up in Rohtak, Haryana. My father was employed in Haryana Government school system, first as a Lecturer and then as a Principal. My mother is a homemaker. Most of the other members in my extended family are either farmers or soldiers.

- As with anyone else, my upbringing has made a huge impact on the choice of my career, and my personality as a whole. The patriotic environment of my family inspired me to make positive contributions to the cause of development of my country. Both my parents often talked about the myriad hardships they faced when they worked on the farms in their youth.
- As I grew older, I figured out that getting into the civil services was the single most effective and efficient way to contribute to the development of the nation while improving the lives of the most vulnerable and disadvantaged sections of the society at the same time. By the time, I was 12, I had a clarity regarding my aim in life.
- My father, being a teacher himself, guided me academically during my school and brought the best out of me. Unfortunately, he passed away in 2011 when I was in Class XI. It was a tough time but I fought the circumstances and managed to come out of it stronger and more independent than ever.
- I wasn't particularly interested in pursuing engineering but had to do so due to the circumstances prevailing in my family. My mother and sisters insisted on having this fall-back mechanism in case I was not able to clear the 'tough' UPSC exam.
- My college life at BITS Pilani, Goa Campus was fun and lively. I got an exposure to the brilliant students and teachers from all across the country, all with their own wonderful visions and missions. The pool of talented hardworking students and their goals in life served as an inspiration to me. The late night debates and discussions with my friends opened me up to new insights on various issues and made me appreciate the beauty of diversity. Despite my initial reluctance to pursue engineering, my experience at the college had a very positive influence on me.
- As the final year of the college dawned, I decided not to sit for the placements, despite reservations expressed by my mother and other well-

wishers. However, I had my mind made up for a long time and decided to prepare for the prestigious Civil Services Examination (CSE) with an 'All in or nothing' attitude.

- After I was done with my college in 2017, I started preparing for the exam and appeared for the CSE 2018. I was fortunate enough to secure All India Rank 374 in the first attempt at a young age of 22, while relying on self-study. This feat could not have been possible without the clarity, passion, self-confidence and courage displayed by me and the support provided by my family and a small but an admirable circle of friends.

Message to Newcomers

- My message to anyone reading this is short and clear: if you have an aim set in your mind, work hard to achieve it. Things will occasionally go bad during the course of your journey, but there's nothing which can't be overcome by determination, grit, hard-work and perseverance.

❑❑

36

Name: Yashraj Nain
Rank: 382, CSE-2018

"UPSC is very unpredictable. While unpredictability is there to a degree, it can be minimised through smart preparation; minimum sources, maximum revisions, solving test papers and courage in the exam hall."

YASHRAJ NAIN

OPTIONAL SUBJECT
Political Science and International Relations

MEDIUM
English

NATIVE PLACE
Jhunjhunu

EDUCATIONAL QUALIFICATION
❖ BA in Economics and Political Science from Hindu College and MA in International Relations from JNU.

COACHING TAKEN
❖ No

MAINS MARKS AND PERSONALITY TEST
Essay (Paper I): 122
General Studies- I (Paper II): 085
General Studies- II (Paper III): 093
General Studies- III (Paper IV): 087
General Studies- IV (Paper V): 108
Optional - I(PS & IR) (Paper VI)-153
Optional - II (PS & IR) (Paper VII)- 171
Written Total- 819 Personality Test- 165 ❖ Final Total: 984

MY JOURNEY

- My study plan was very erratic. I didn't have fixed schedule and lacked consistency. Sometimes I won't feel like studying for days on end.
- This is obviously not recommended.
- At the same time those of you who struggle to put in the magical 6 hours or more daily shouldn't lose hope. A lot of people have aced this exam without that.

Message for Newcomers:

- At the risk of sounding cliched, I must say that there is no substitute for consistency and hard work.
- Having said that, one should never feel overwhelmed or anxious about his preparedness level. The exam tests so many diverse traits of an individual that even if immediate academic preparation is less, one can still ace it.
- Many newcomers feel that UPSC is very unpredictable. While unpredictability is there to a degree, it can be minimised through smart preparation; minimum sources, maximum revisions, solving test papers and courage in the exam hall.
- Selection of optional subject is very important. It can make or mar your result. Thus one must choose carefully based one's aptitude and interest.
- Both essay and interview carry a wide range in terms of score. They are crucial in getting an edge over the competition.
- I tried to write an essay every fortnight. I jotted down a number of quotes from eminent thinkers and tried to assimilate them in my essays.
- Similarly, systematic interview preparation is very crucial. This is often neglected by newcomers.
- I had college seniors who got selected and they helped me a lot in navigating the exam process. The guidance they provided proved invaluable. If one doesn't have direct guidance then blogs of toppers are readily available on the internet. These should be read to get a better idea about various challenges in the exam and ways of overcoming them. I benefitted from Youtube videos and blogs posted by various previous years' toppers.

❑❑

37

Name: Garima Dahiya
Rank: 394, CSE-2018

"Have faith in yourself with a clear sense of goal and commitment with relentless persistence. You will ace this exam."

GARIMA DAHIYA

OPTIONAL SUBJECT
Geography

MEDIUM
English

NATIVE PLACE
Sisana, Sonipat (Haryana)

EDUCATIONAL QUALIFICATION
❖ BSc (H)Physics

PARENTS' OCCUPATION
❖ **Father:** Assistant Sub Inspector
❖ **Mother:** Homemaker

COACHING TAKEN
❖ No

MARKS
Prelims: Paper -1: 108.66 and Paper -125

MAINS MARKS AND PERSONALITY TEST
Essay (Paper I): 112
General Studies- I (Paper II): 101
General Studies- II (Paper III): 105
General Studies- III (Paper IV): 102
General Studies- IV (Paper V): 105
Optional - I (Geography) (Paper VI)-136
Optional - II (Geography (Paper VII) - 131
Written Total- 792 Personality Test- 190 ❖ Final Total: 982

MY JOURNEY

UPSC journey in itself is a time taking process and it's very natural that there will be gamut of challenges not just related to this exam but also related to your personal life.

So, in my case this was my 3rd attempt. I had cleared prelims in every attempt.But I missed my mains in 2016 by 32 marks and In 2017 by 13 marks. At that time, I was just shattered. But then I again gained strength and started preparation as I had this very clear in my mind that this was my decision to prepare for this exam and this was the only thing which I wanted to do.

In my third attempt, I faced a different set of challenges. Just before 10 days from mains examination, we faced an extreme health emergency in our family.During all that time I was in the hospital and was thinking not to give examination. That was the most difficult phase of my life and I had sleepless nights. But some of my friends instilled a sense of confidence in me and I gave mains. During that time, daily it was a sort of journey from examination centre to hospital.But I was determined and did not want to succumb to challenges.

After mains I was not expecting an interview call as my essay and optional papers were really bad and specially in optional paper 2, I couldn't even complete the paper due to high physical and mental fatigue. But with Almighty's wish and prayers of my family and friends I could find my name in the final list.

Book List

I am not sharing a proper booklist as one can find it from toppers' videos. But I will say few words of caution

- Have a continuous look at the syllabus and previous years' papers.
- Analyse the previous years papers properly.
- Keep your sources limited.
- Read less and revise more and more.
- Have a good peer group.
- Add some form of physical and mental exercise in your daily routine to keep yourself healthy.

Message for Newcomers

I am a strong believer in "WHAT DOES NOT KILL YOU, MAKES YOU STRONGER". So, every experience counts in our life. Specially the hard experiences gives us a better sense of learning at times. So take these hard experiences as a learning curve. As this examination tests suitability of a candidate at various stages and looks for the different tenets of our personality. So have faith in yourself with a clear sense of goal and commitment with relentless persistence.

And finally

As they say "Tundi-e- Baad-E-Mukhalif se na ghabra, ae Uqaab, Yeh to chalti hai tujhe uncha udane ke liye".

❑❑

38

Name: Hitesh Kumar Meena

Rank: 417, CSE-2018, Rank-54, IFS-2018

"Work with confidence, you will surely get success"

HITESH KUMAR MEENA

OPTIONAL SUBJECT

Civil Engineering

MEDIUM

English

NATIVE PLACE

Karauli (Rajasthan)

EDUCATIONAL QUALIFICATION

❖ B Btech (IIT BHU Varanasi) & Mtech (IIT Delhi)

PARENTS' OCCUPATION

❖ **Father:** (Harirram Meena): Government Teacher

❖ **Mother:** (Sarwati Meena): Homemaker

COACHING TAKEN

❖ GS by self study(coaching for optional and test series) ; Struggle part – it was my 3rd attempt

MARKS

Prelims: Paper -1: 106.00 and Paper -119.18

MAINS MARKS AND PERSONALITY TEST

Essay (Paper I): 119

General Studies- I (Paper II): 107

General Studies- II (Paper III): 113

General Studies- III (Paper IV): 106

General Studies- IV (Paper V): 113

Optional - I (Civil Engineering) (Paper VI)-132

Optional - II (Civil Engineering) (Paper VII)- 158

Written Total- 848 Personality Test- 129 ❖ Final Total: 977

My father Hariram Meena is a teacher in a government school in Rajaur village and my mother is housewife. My grandparents are farmers. I grew up in a middle class family with a rustic atmosphere. I started my education in Rajiv Gandhi school located at my Village and then I came to Kota for coaching after passing 12th standard from a private school in Karauli. I got selected in IIT and completed B.Tech in Varanasi. When I was doing IIT in Varanasi, then the idea of serving the poor backward class people came to my mind, who have not the fortune of a helping hand. IAS service is considered better for this. Through this service my intention is to help such people, who are deprived of wealth, bread and clothes. Being backward in every respect and who is really needy person don't get the benefits of government schemes.

I got selected in IAS in the third attempt. I have 417th rank in the country whereas, got fifth rank in Scheduled Tribes category. Prior to this, there was a second time selection in IFS. I got the first rank in the Scheduled Tribes category and 54th in All India. Recently I completed M.Tech from Delhi.

And as far as regular studies are concerned, I had not made any hard and fast rule to study regularly, but during the examination, I used to study for about 15 hours a day. On average, I have studied for 7 to 8 hours daily .

MY SINCERE MESSAGE FOR PEOPLE PREPARING FOR CIVIL EXAMS

First of all, for any success it is necessary to keep your confidence strong. If you don't get the success at first time don't get disappointed, understand the syllabus very well. Solve old papers, take it easy not like a burden. Don't miss to take the guidance from your seniors while preparing and take full enjoy of study. Always make big goals, each one has infinite abilities. It is important to follow the essence of Gita. Do not worry about fruits. Social media should be used positively. I used it fully while preparation, took help in getting new information and continue taking the guidance from seniors. Young people should use these platform and resources in materializing their goals.

❑❑❑

39

Name: Anil Kumar Jhajharia
Rank: 431, CSE-2018

"Do not lose hope if the result is not in your favour. Just keep going. Brace yourself for a long battle."

ANIL KUMAR JHAJHARIA

OPTIONAL SUBJECT
Sociology

MEDIUM
English

NATIVE PLACE
Sikar (Rajasthan)

EDUCATIONAL QUALIFICATION
❖ B.Tech – IIT Mandi (2015)

PARENTS' OCCUPATION
❖ **Father:** Head Constable in Delhi Police
❖ **Mother:** Homemaker

COACHING TAKEN
❖ Sociology – Nice IAS
❖ GS – None

MARKS
Prelims: Paper -1: 100 and Paper -2: Don't Remember

MAINS MARKS AND PERSONALITY TEST
Essay (Paper I): 118
General Studies- I (Paper II): 105
General Studies- II (Paper III): 112
General Studies- III (Paper IV): 095
General Studies- IV (Paper V): 098
Optional - I (Sociology) (Paper VI)-130
Optional - II (Sociology) (Paper VII)- 138
Written Total- 796 Personality Test- 178 ❖ Final Total: 974

MY JOURNEY

How to overcome the ups/down

Initial few days are the hardest. I dropped out of my Masters to prepare for the CSE. And there weren't many backups available for me at that time in case of failure. Also, most of us have no idea about what, why, when etc, of this exam. At that time, it's very easy to lose the sight or overwhelmed by the hype of CSE. At such times, be patient and keep going. If necessary, take guidance from seniors, teachers, and friends.

I was lucky enough to reach the CSE interview stage in all my three attempts, however, when I didn't see my name in the final merit list in the first attempt, it was a big let down for me. But the next Prelims exam was a few days away, and I had to focus on that. At that time, friends and parents helped me a lot. So be patient, and do not hesitate to take help. Also, take a short break after Prelims to recharge your batteries before Mains.

At last, take it as just another exam. Frankly, I've seen more people clearing this exam when they became slightly detached. So please let's not be too obsessed with it.

List of Books

- Art and Culture: Book by Nitin Singhania
- GS -2: Pawan Kumar's notes, ARC Reports' summary, Vision IAS booklets
- GS -3: mainly VisionIAS booklets, M K Yadav's notes
- GS 4: ARC's 4th report, made my own notes from internet
- Interview: internet and newspapers

Message for Newcomers

- Some brief points to which for newcomers can consider are:
- Understand the exam, know the syllabus and pattern/mode of examination. Refer to previous years' question papers.
- Write mock test papers for both Prelims and Mains examination.
- For GS papers: prepare short notes/ 1-page notes on each topic of the syllabus (will help a lot in Mains exam)
- If something doesn't work for you, review it and change it.
- Finally, don't lose hope if the result is not in your favour. Just keep going. Brace yourself for a long battle.

❑❑

40

Name: Satyanarayan Prajapat
Rank: 445, CSE-2018

"Civil service exam can be a long journey which will have many ups and downs. In difficult phases, it is very important to keep yourself motivated and maintain a positive mindset."

SATYANARAYAN PRAJAPAT

OPTIONAL SUBJECT
Sociology

MEDIUM
English

NATIVE PLACE
Sujangarh, Churu (Rajasthan)

EDUCATIONAL QUALIFICATION
- B. Tech in Chemical Engineering from NIT Warangal

PARENTS' OCCUPATION
- **Father:** Mason, Agriculturist
- **Mother:** Home Maker, Agriculturist

COACHING TAKEN
- Preparation Self-study, Vision IAS Test series for GS, NICE IAS Test series for Sociology optional

MARKS
Prelims: Paper -1: 126 and Paper -2: 116

MAINS MARKS AND PERSONALITY TEST
Essay (Paper I): 110
General Studies- I (Paper II): 082
General Studies- II (Paper III): 112
General Studies- III (Paper IV): 103
General Studies- IV (Paper V): 105
Optional - I (Sociology) (Paper, VI)-165
Optional - II (Sociology) (Paper VII)- 133
Written Total- 810 Personality Test- 160 ❖ Final Total: 970

MY JOURNEY

(a) Struggle Part :

Preparation for UPSC Civil Service Examination (CSE) demand two things – time and patience, along with other qualities. And if you are a working professional, then finding adequate time for your studies is always a challenge.

Since I decided to prepare to CSE while being in the job, I had limited time for the studies. So it became crucial that I utilize whatever free time I had, particularly on weekend. I also tried to utilize the free time during office hours to read the newspaper and magazine. In retrospect, I believe that it is possible to clear CSE while working simultaneously, however maintaining consistency is always a challenge.

Time management becomes more crucial when you have a plenty of material available to read. Now a days, when there is so much online and offline study material available, selection of what to read becomes important. Restricting yourself to read the selected material is also challenging.

Next crucial factor that determines the outcome of our preparation is to know what exactly UPSC is demanding from aspirants. In my first attempt in 2016, I had prepared the static part very well for the Prelims. However, I was not able to figure out that UPSC has started asking current affairs a lot and I had to pay the price for my ignorance.

After my first failed attempt, I figured out that more time needs to be given to maintain consistency and for practice. However there was one constrain that I could not afford to be out of job for a long time. That is the time when we have to take a call and put our best efforts in order to prove that we took the right call. I decided to take paid leave 4 months before the prelims exam in 2017.

By rectifying the earlier mistakes, I was able to score decently in Prelims 2017, however I had not prepared the optional subject till then. So a most part of the time between prelims and mains went in preparing the optional. Here I made another mistake by not giving sufficient time to all the subjects and not writing test series for GS subjects. That also got reflected in the mark sheet and fell 12 marks short from cutoff marks. However I tried to rectify these mistakes in my third attempt and was able to secure a rank by God's grace. Identifying our shortcomings and devising an appropriate strategy to overcome them is the most crucial challenge in our journey to success in CSE.

- Other than these challenges, I faced one more challenge which was to supplement my father's income and take care of the financial needs of my four younger siblings' study even when I was not earning. In those difficult times, it were my friends who came to my rescue and they helped my generously. It was this time when I realized how important it is to have a group of supportive friends. I am heavily indebted to those friends.

(b) Book List

- Art and Culture: Nitin Singhania
- Ancient history: Old NCERTs (R S Sharma)
- Medieval: Old NCERT (Satish Chandra)
- Modern History: Spectrum (Rajiv Ahir)
- Polity: Laxmikanth
- Environment: Shankar IAS
- Economics: Sriram's economy notes
- Geography: Class 9-12 NCERTs
- Current Affairs: Reading one national newspaper (preferably Indian Express/ The Hindu), monthly/ annually current affairs compilations of Vision IAS/ Insights.

Vision IAS's Value added material is useful for covering Indian Society, Disaster management, National security and Ethics.

Message for newcomers

- Previous year's question papers: UPSC CSE is somewhat different from other competitive exams. It does not require that an aspirant should do all the things. However UPSC tests general understanding of the issues which have direct socio-political and economic implication. New candidates should constantly see the previous years' Prelims and Mains question papers and figure out why a particular question has been asked.
- Practicing mock papers: is very crucial for both Prelims and Mains.
- Key to success in prelims is revising static part from same source supplemented with current affairs and practising as many mock papers as possible.
- For Mains, allocating adequate time to all subjects including essay and ethics is crucial. Joining a test series helps in improving the structure of

the answers and better understand the demand of the question. It also helps in better time management during final examination.

- Constant Motivation: As it is well known, UPSC CSE can be a long journey which will have many ups and downs. In difficult phases, it is very important to keep yourself motivated and maintain a positive mindset. Family, friends, motivational talks can become your source of inspiration.
- Learning from mistakes: figuring out our shortcomings and rectifying them is the most important aspect in achieving success.

❑❑

41

Name: Lokesh Yadav
Rank: 452, CSE-2018

"UPSC is a marathon not a 100 metre sprint so discover for yourself the ideal pace which can be maintained for a period of over an year."

LOKESH YADAV

OPTIONAL SUBJECT

Management

MEDIUM

English

NATIVE PLACE

Rewari District, Haryana

EDUCATIONAL QUALIFICATION

❖ B.Tech → IIT Delhi (2015)

❖ MBA→ IIM Ahmedabad (2017)

PARENTS' OCCUPATION

❖ **Father:** Sub Division Officer in thermal power station, Hisar

❖ **Mother:** Home Maker

COACHING TAKEN

❖ GS, ALS Coaching Institute

MARKS

Prelims: Paper -1: 104 and Paper -2: 156

MAINS MARKS AND PERSONALITY TEST

Essay (Paper I): 125

General Studies- I (Paper II): 092

General Studies- II (Paper III): 102

General Studies- III (Paper IV): 103

General Studies- IV (Paper V): 93

Management Optional: 293

Interview: 160

MY JOURNEY/STRUGGLE

- With God's grace and blessing of my parents, near and dear ones, I was able to clear this prestigious exam in the very 1st attempt. However, my journey also had it's share of ups and downs.
- I had it somewhere in the back of my mind from childhood to give this exam at least one shot in my life. However, I hadn't given it a serious enough thought till my post graduation.
- During my intern at Goldman Sachs in my post graduation, I dwelled upon the idea of working in the private sector vs a public sector and the sustainability and impact I could create in both the professions. Be it as investment banker vs a bureaucrat.
- With some weeks of introspection and contemplating, I decided to take a plunge and started my preparation for UPSC in mid 2017 right after my post graduation from IIM Ahmedabad.
- The initial few months went in building the basics and figuring out what are the bare minimum requirements of the exam and what is the right approach and frame of mind towards the examination in particular and this profession in general.
- Two major reasons for my success were:
  1. Restricting my sources to a bare minimum, either due to paucity of time or consciously → I applied it across prelims, mains as well as interview.
  2. Convincing and having utmost faith in your capabilities → If you yourself cannot believe that you will clear this exam, then how will others believe?
- I tried to evaluate everything I did on the cost benefit analysis parameter i.e. given the time, I am devoting how much return it would fetch me in the exam → using this metric prioritising my study material.

RECOMMENDED SOURCES/BOOKS

- Polity: M.Laxmikant, M. Puri sir's notes
- History:Spectrum
- Economics: Budget and Economic Survey synopsis/summary
- Art and culture: Nitin Singhania, NCERT fine arts book
- Geography: G.C. Leong

- Ethics: 2nd ARC ethics and governance
- Management: Organisational behaviour by Niharika Vohra, Marketing by Kotler

Message for the Newcomers

- UPSC is a marathon, not a 100m sprint so discover for yourself the ideal pace which can be maintained for a period of over an year
- Have a regular feedback loop for yourself to evaluate where you stand vis-a-vis your goal → through regular testing [test series come in handy here]
- Learn from each mistake of yours and try to amend it in the next exam
- Always remember, the one who sweats in practice bleeds less in war
- Apply Pareto principle i.e. 20% of the things carry 80% of the weight hence prioritise to get maximum return
- I would repeat the cliché but correct statement that "Read a book 10 times than reading 10 books."
- Finally believe in yourself and your success along with never being afraid of failure.

42

Name: Vikas Marmat
Rank: 473, 12th (ST), CSE, 2018

"Trust yourself, trust your sources, trust your teachers, trust your parents, trust your God because when you trust, you gain confidence and when you are confident, no one can stop you from performing your best."

VIKAS MARMAT

OPTIONAL SUBJECT
Sociology

MEDIUM
English

NATIVE PLACE
Jaipur, Rajasthan

EDUCATIONAL QUALIFICATIONS
B.tech in Mechanical Engineering, 2017

MARKS
Prelims Score: GS – 103, CSAT - 140

MAINS MARKS AND PERSONALITY TEST
Essay (Paper I): 102
General Studies- I (Paper II): 089
General Studies- II (Paper III): 112
General Studies- III (Paper IV): 089
General Studies- IV (Paper V): 097
Optional - I (Sociology) (Paper VI): 164
Optional - II (Sociology) (Paper VII): 128
Written Total: 781
Personality Test: 182
Final Total: 963

MY JOURNEY

Life is full of surprises and you have to embrace every surprise with a positive gratitude and attitude. I went to IIT Kanpur with the motivation that I'll grab a good job and earn decent money but my destiny had some other plans. In our college, we had to do 5 compulsory courses in humanities whereby I chose 3 courses of sociology. I got too much involved in Sociology as I got to study all of those things which I use to see in my daily life from a new angle. Finally, I decided to do something at the ground level and civil services was one of the options. I completed reading of all the NCERT textbooks and some standard books like *spectrum* in college itself. At first, I was thinking to give exam in 2017 itself but I couldn't prepare very well in college as I had no good guidance. I decided to go to Delhi while some people told me about the problems students face in Delhi. When I discussed it with my parents, they told me that if I really want to clear this exam then you should be ready to face anything that comes in my way. It hit me hard and thus my mind was well prepared for the adversities of preparation phase while living in Delhi, which helped me in sustaining the pressure of competition, pollution, food of Delhi etc.

As far as my struggle is considered, there are 3 points that I would like to mention. Firstly, I was not well versed with English and many people told me that a decent fluency in English is necessary to write good answers as well as to crack the interview so I started focusing on it. I started to speak in English with most of my friends and also started reading English newspapers in my college. Secondly, I was a B.Tech student, thus had no idea about the humanities' subjects which made it really difficult to take a decision whereby I was required to read the latter subjects. It was all together a challenge to study all of that which I had left in class 10th but the zeal to explore these subjects was strong enough to make me comfortable with it. Thirdly, I used to be very much active on social media in my college days but I deactivated my Facebook account, Instagram account, changed my number on WhatsApp, did not attend any family functions thus I left the world I was addicted to. One has to be strong enough to sacrifice some of the habits which acts as an obstacle in one's way. Trust me, the fruits of the sacrifices will be very sweet and worth eating.

Message for Newcomers

I once read that 'in the battle of life, not the faster or stronger women wins; but the person who wins is the one who thinks she can'. These lines conclude that confidence is an important key to success. Further, confidence without strategy and planning is of no use i.e. proper study plan + material + guidance is equally important. Study for atleast 10-12 hours a day in your preparation phase and if need be, join a good coaching as well. UPSC is an exam of attitude more than one's aptitude i.e. one shouldn't be afraid of huge syllabus or low marks in test series etc. but yes one should take them seriously. Syllabus is the bible, which helps in carving out important topics from the various books, newspapers etc. Further in test series, working on your weak topics and rebounding in the next test should become a norm for an aspirant. While preparing, one must be aware of the seriousness of the friends he/she is preparing with, for example if your friend is asking you to visit malls, watch movies etc. then you must realize that his/her's friendship is an obstacle for realizing your dreams. Some of the other suggestions are:

- ❖ Join a good coaching if you left studying arts subjects in class 10th otherwise it will become difficult to understand what to study and what not to.
- ❖ Make a group of serious friends and discuss the newspapers/other topics with them. Try to discuss it in English and try to learn from other person's opinions.
- ❖ Prelims or mains or interview, at every stage - practice as many tests/ mock interviews as you can. Remember that scores or reviews of these tests should be considered only as a way to improve and not something to cry upon.
- ❖ Never ignore any topic based on its weightage in previous year question papers. We don't know what UPSC will focus upon in the upcoming papers. Always study everything that needs to be studied.
- ❖ A week/day before your examination - trust yourself, trust your sources, trust your teachers, trust your parents, trust your God because when you trust, you gain confidence and when you are confident, no one can stop you from performing your best.

At last, I would like to say that there can be thousand reasons for not being able to do it but you should find that one reason about why you want to do it and trust me, you'll do it. If you really want to clear this exam, you will, no one else can decide it for you other than hard work and perseverance.

❑❑

43

Name: Hemant Kumar Meena
Rank: 532, CSE 2018

"Believe in yourself, there may be low phases in your preparation, but you need to be strong in those times and remember why you came here in the first place."

HEMANT KUMAR MEENA

OPTIONAL SUBJECT
Geography

MEDIUM
English

NATIVE PLACE
Ranauli, Karauli dist, Rajasthan

EDUCATIONAL QUALIFICATIONS
B.Tech. IIT Roorkee (2013)

PARENTS OCCUPATION
❖ **Father** : Govt employee ❖ **Mother** : Homemaker

COACHING TAKEN
❖ **GS** : Vajiram & Ravi
❖ **Geography:** ALS (would not recommend it)

MARKS
105(GS paper 1)

MAINS MARKS AND PERSONALITY TEST
Essay (Paper I): 134
General Studies- I (Paper II): 091
General Studies- II (Paper III): 109
General Studies- III (Paper IV): 098
General Studies- IV (Paper V): 099
Optional - I (Geography) (Paper VI): 120
Optional - II (Geography) (Paper VII): 129
Written Total: 780
Personality Test: 171
Final Total: 951

MY JOURNEY

Seeds of Civil Service

Examination were sown in me during my school days itself, though they were in a latent state till my graduation. After graduation at IIT Roorkee, I came to Delhi for coaching and preparation.

The first issue I faced was in **deciding the medium** of examination, since my school education was in Hindi medium but my college education was in English medium. After reading NCERT books in both the mediums, I decided to choose English. I had to struggle a lot on this front but eventually it turned out to be a right choice for me.

Then **deciding an optional** was not an easy task. Initially, I wanted to opt for chemistry, which was my area of interest during my B.Tech years. But after discussions with some friends and seniors, I decided to go with Geography. As Geography covers almost half of GS paper1 and there is less guidance for chemistry (which is not really true as I found out later). Sometimes, I regret that I should have chosen chemistry as an optional as it was my area of interest.

So my advice to all the aspirants - choose your optional wisely, your interest matters and so does smart preparation, I caution aspirants to not blindly follow your friends and seniors in choosing optionals as some subject may work for others but it may not work for you.

After this, my journey of CSE preparation started in Delhi. I was fortunate enough to write the mains examination in 2014 itself. I missed the cutoff by 50 marks. Here lies my biggest mistake, not introspecting what went wrong in the preparation of my optional subject, which was my weak point. Because of it, I paid the price again in 2015 Mains.

After this, I rectified my mistakes of GS papers. And I gave my first interview in 2016 by clearing mains cutoff by small margin. But I missed the final cutoff by arround 25 marks.

Then I failed in CSE mains 2017, which was devastating for me.I started doubting my strategy and myself. My confidence was very low at this point. But it turned out to be a turning point in my journey of CSE.

This is the time where you need all kinds of support - from your family, your friends & most importantly from within yourself. My family supported me in those tough times especially- my bade papa and my elder cousin.

After this, I introspected my strategy, I found my optional as the reason for my failure.Then I decided to change my optional to Sociology. But after studying it, I realised that every subject has its nitty gritties. No optional is easy, though there may be a variation in length of syllabus, nature of paper & marking pattern.

Eventually I decided to work on Geography by consulting my friends, who had scored good marks.

Then the attempt of CSE 2018, the stakes were very high. But, I worked harder and smarter than ever. Fortunately, hard work paid off and I scored AIR 532.

This reaffirms my belief in hard work and dedication towards achieving one's goal in life.

LIST OF BOOKS

Message for Newcomers

- Believe in yourself, there may be low phases in your preparation, but you need to be strong in those times & remember why you came here in the first place.
- Ask yourself 'if others can do it, why can't you?'
- Lastly a message as my father says - 'Samay se pehle aur bhagya se zyada kuchh nahi milta.' So be patient & study.

❑❑

44

Name: Sparsh Gupta
Rank: 562, CSE-2018

"I believe that self belief, dedication and determination are the three components of success in this journey. You have to trust that the methods that have taken you so far in your life will continue to reap rewards in this journey as well."

SPARSH GUPTA

OPTIONAL SUBJECT
Law

MEDIUM
English

NATIVE PLACE
Bulandshahar, Uttar Pradesh, 203001

EDUCATIONAL QUALIFICATION
❖ B.A.,LL.B (Hons.) from National Law School of India University, Bangalore

PARENTS' OCCUPATION
❖ **Father:** Chartered Accountant (CA)
❖ **Mother:** Homemaker

COACHING TAKEN
❖ **Prelims:** Vision IAS Test Serries
❖ **General Studies and Law Optional:** Nirvana IAS Academy
❖ **Interview:** Nirvana IAS, Vision IAS and Samkalp IAS Academy

MARKS
❖ GS1: 75.66
❖ GS2: 136.66

MAINS MARKS AND PERSONALITY TEST
❖ GS1: 86
❖ GS2: 103
❖ GS3: 83
❖ GS4: 95
❖ Essay: 135
❖ Optional Paper1: 144
❖ Optional paper2: 142

CONTACT
Facebook- https://www.facebook.com/sparsh.nls.bng?ref=bookmarks

MY JOURNEY

My journey for Civil Services began in 2016 when I had undergone surgery on my right eye for Glaucoma. This was the time when I had lost all hope as I had been gradually losing vision in my eyes and constantly making adjustments for doing my daily chores and the problems were making me doubt myself. This was also the time when I got an opportunity to self-introspect and decide what do I want to do in the future. I had two options, continue with the private law firm job which was paying me well or to secure my future. After a lot of introspection, I gathered courage and took the plunge and jumped into the field of Civil Services Exam. My parents and close friends were a big reason that I could take such a decision despite all odds working against me.

To be honest, I had no dream of going into Civil Services from childhood. A lot of my family friends used to recommend me to write this exam as I was always good with academics but I never paid heed to them till 2014. It was during the 4th year of my college that I had an honest discussion with my friend who was writing this exam and tried to understand the process. But, there was no further progress at that time also and I decided to give private job one shot and see how things go from there. But, as the destiny would have it, I landed up into the CSE field at last.

Being a differently abled has its own challenges. Life before was not easy at all and knowing CSE being such a difficult exam, it was doubly difficult for me. But, my parents, specially my mother had always told me since childhood that “Beta, nothing can stop you from what you have once decided in life not even this disability and give it your all and you will be a role model for rest of the society.” Those were the words which kept me motivated throughouts highs and lows of this journey.

Firstly, it was so difficult initially to get hold of the material which was accessible. A little bit of a background, so for people who cannot see or are printly disabled, there is a technology called text to speech which converts text into readable speech. I had done my college studies also using these softwares. But, for these softwares to be useful, the documents must be in a text form for it to be compatible. And a lot of the material was not available in readable formats. So, I had to find solutions for the same. This was a big problem specially while collecting material for law optional. So, almost the whole of my first attempt went in compilling reading sources which were compatible with my softwares.

This was my first attempt and I had written Mains three times but unfortunately I could not clear Mains the first two times. It was very frustrating not to qualify the Mains especially the second time around. But, my parents and close friends always motivated me that you have it in you and it's just a matter of little more hardwork and you will sail through. But, after the second attempt, I decided to join regular coaching and moved to Delhi for the last attempt. I joined Nirvana IAS and that was where I shone through like a diamond. It was Gill Sir at Nirvana who mentored me and I was finally able to clear this exam. One important difference that I can identify this time around was that my preparation was more robust and meticulous and since we rely more on hearing and hence attending regular classes and writing decent amount of mocks really helped me. One big challenge for me was also to be able to dictate answers and compatibility with my scribe who was our reader and writer for the exam. For the first two times, I took Commission's scribe but having realised the hurdles in coordination and problems in terms of logistics, I felt that I should take my own scribe this time around. And it paid dividends handsomely as my results showed.

In the end, I can say, it is not an easy exam at all and it is a long marathon that you have to constantly keep pace with. One mis-step and you could end up wasting one whole year. The uncertainty and vagaries of this exam are such that you should always have an alternate career plan in your mind. Like after having missed the list twice, I joined ONGC as Assistant Legal Advisor to keep myself occupied. Further, constant support from my parents, close friends, my scribe's efforts, despite her poor health and excellent mentorship by Gill sir enabled me to pass this exam with flying colors.

These lines describe my journey best- "Lehron se darker nauka paar nahi hoti, koshish karne walon ki kabhi haar nahi hoti" So, keep working towards your goals and you will achieve some day.

My message to newcomers

Self belief, dedication and determination. I believe these are the three components of success in this journey. You have to trust that the methods that have taken you so far in life will continue to reap rewards in this journey as well. The biggest blunder that aspirants make in this exam is that they consult too many sources instead of focussing on quality and building on their knowledge by constant revision. Also, one more thing one should keep in mind is that you shouldn't get influenced by so many toppers' strategies. These are good anecdotes to get motivated but only take that part of their strategy which suits you and do not follow it blindly. For instance, most toppers say they used to study for 12-15 hours a day, I knew from beginning that I wouldn't be able to do that and if tried to do it, I will exhaust myself and would do more harm than benefitting myself. Hence, I used to study for 8 hours a day but with 100% productivity and consistency.

In conclusion, this journey is just a test of you mental strength and nothing else. Also, keep in mind, it's just an exam and not the end of your life. It is just a means to achieve a goal in life and not an end in itself. The main struggle begins once you get into the service and step out into the real playground called the 'Indian Administration'

❑❑

45

Name: Jagdish Kumar
Rank: 564, CSE-2018

Nothing is impossible! You can do what you think and achieve that too!

JAGDISH KUMAR

OPTIONAL SUBJECT
History

MEDIUM
Hindi

NATIVE PLACE
Munthala Kaaba; Bhinmal; Jalore (Rajasthan)
(Jalore is an educationally backward districts in Rajasthan)

EDUCATIONAL QUALIFICATION
- BA (Hons-History) (Goldmedalist) -2012; MA (History) 2014; PhD (Researched since January 2016) Jai Narayan Vyas University, Jodhpur (Rajasthan)

PRE-SELECTION
UGC NET / JRF (June 2014), Assistant Commandant (CAPF / AC) (2015)

PARENTS' OCCUPATION
- **Father:** (was a farmer) died in 2009
- **Mother:** Housewife

COACHING TAKEN
General Studies (Paper 1, 2, 3): Mission IAS
Essays and Ethics
Dhyeya IAS and Drishti the Vision IAS

TEST SERIES
Vision IAS

MARKS

Prelims: Paper -1: General Studies 1: 98.66

Paper -2: General Studies 2: 106

MAINS MARKS AND PERSONALITY TEST

Essay (Paper I): 139

General Studies- I (Paper II): 072

General Studies- II (Paper III): 099

General Studies- III (Paper IV): 076

General Studies- IV (Paper V): 091

Optional - I (History) (Paper VI)-152

Optional - II (History) (Paper VII)- 152

Total Marks of Main Examination: 775

Interview: 173

Total Marks: 948

MY JOURNEY

This is exactly ten years ago. In the year 2000, I had a major turning point in my life. My dad died prematurely just before my 12th board exam. For the first time in his life, it was an unreplaceable loss. Since I was the youngest in the family, I was also the closest to my father. Due to this shock, life stopped for some time. After my board exams, the right marks also came, that's why I took admission in BA (Hons-History) at Jodhpur University . Now my main dream was to take a job as soon as possible. I don't know anything about UPSC. Laxminarayan Ji sir (Assistant Professor, Economics, Jodhpur) showed the dream of UPSC, Guided and encouraged me regularly.

In 2013, the first prelims was a failure, so the effort was doubled. 2014 CSE Interviewed but did not get success. This series of pre mains and interviews CSE. In 2018, the sixth attempt broke through and my name finally came on the final list, I had worked tirelessly for the past several years.

How to handle yourself in constant failure?

In the midst of scorching heat of UPSC preparations, some small success showers of rain did not let it get tired. Also unconditional support of family and elder brother; Vinay Singhji sir With the support of Laxmi Narayan ji sir, Shishtaji Jain sir (IAS) and friends, I always kept getting new energy.

Credo of success

Work with honesty, dedication to the goal, maintain patience and from the mistakes of yourself and others, learning, practicing writing continuously, revising again and again.

The mistakes I made: not practicing writing, being casual about the essay (so every simple mark in the essay every time), following a lot of sources, in history paper do not practice mapping.

Books and Botes

History: Ancient India- Upendra Singh, took the help of Google for mapping.

Medieval India- Notes of Harish Chandra Varma, Hemant Jha Sir.

Notes of Modern India-Shekhar Bandopadhyay, Manikant Sir.

Notes of World History-Jain & Mathur, Manikant Sir.

Basic Book for General Studies (Unacademy of Nisht Jain Sir for detailed information)

Must see video) and value addition notes of vision Ias Syllabus Topics

Notes of the IAS and Vision IAS according to repeatedly read the essay written by the toppers for the essay. Quotes and examples wherever you find it, write it in a notebook.

The message for the candidates should be to prepare UPSC not only to become an IAS, but to be a meaningful person. This will make the journey of preparation fantastic. Work hard but keep your attention and put your energy in the right direction. The practice of writing can prove to be a panacea in preparation. As well as others must learn from the mistakes of Continuing your preparation with the test series for the pre exam keep evaluating. Taking CSAT paper lightly can spoil your one year.Do write 2-3 essays in a month. Write at least 2 answers in the optional subject every day. Do not get habitually addicted to social media (FB, Instagram).

❑❑

46

Name: Devender Singh Chaudhary

Rank: 575 (CSE-2018), 718 (CSE-2016)

"UPSC is a long process, so first of all mentally prepare yourself for this journey. Internal motivation is the biggest driving factor that will keep you going."

DEVENDER SINGH CHAUDHARY

OPTIONAL SUBJECT
Geography

MEDIUM
English

NATIVE PLACE
Village : Bhanoli, Tehsil : Dooni, Dist : Tonk, Rajasthan

WORK EXPERIENCE
Worked in Reliance Industries (Navi Mumbai) from August 2011 to June 2015.

EDUCATIONAL QUALIFICATION
- BE (Electronics & Communication) 2007-2011 from Army Institute of Technology Pune. MTech (Optoelectronics & Optical communication) 2015-2017 from IIT Delhi.

PARENTS' OCCUPATION
- **Father:** Retired as Subedar Major from Army, currently working in Railways.
- **Mother:** Homemaker

COACHING TAKEN
- From ALS IAS (Karol Bagh, Delhi) while pursuing my MTech from IIT Delhi.

MARKS
- **Prelims 2018**

Paper 1 - 102, Paper 2 - 125

MAINS AND INTERVIEW SCORE
Essay (Paper I)- 128
General Studies- I (Paper II)- 091
General Studies- II (Paper III)- 103
General Studies- III (Paper IV)- 101
General Studies- IV (Paper V)- 091
Optional - I (Geography) (Paper VI)-109
Optional - II (Geography) (Paper VII)- 158
Written Total- 781, Personality Test- 165
Final Total- 946

MY JOURNEY

I did not face much struggle if we talk about the financial aspect related to the coaching fees or study material, but because of the long span of the UPSC exam (the process from prelims to mains, interviews and final results takes more than a year), every aspirant faces challenges. I always wanted to work as a public servant (because my grandfather had this dream) but I started preparing very late. I wrote my first prelims in 2014 while I was working in Reliance, didn't prepare much just read NCERT books and some basic books like Bipin Chandra and Laxmikanth. Since I had no one to guide, I was not well prepared and thus failed in prelims. Then I planned to leave my job and go to Delhi to prepare for UPSC, but I had given GATE exam in February 2014, which was valid for 2015 also. So, I appeared for MTech interview and made it to IIT. I joined MTech in July 2015 and along with this I joined UPSC coaching. The real struggle started here because managing classes at college and then GS and Optional coaching was very hectic. The reason of joining MTech was that it would have reduced the stress on my parents regarding the uncertainties about my future and didn't put any financial stress on them (as MTech students get stipend of Rs.12400, if you maintain CGPA above 7 and staying in hostel is any day better than statying outside in ORN). I used to complete my classes in college till 1:30 pm, then rush to metro station Hauz khas to attend optional classes at Karol Bagh from 2 PM- 5PM and then GS classes from 6:30 Pm – 9 Pm. So I spent the whole year following this schedule, missing my dinner at the mess every day (it closed at 9 pm) and eating aalo paratha in the night canteen. Then had to study for quizzes, minor and major exams in order to maintain required CGPA. But I managed to do this because CSE was the dream of my entire family and I was the fortunate one from my village, who was able to get opportunities to work on it. Failure was not an option because I had full support of my parents (who initially wanted me not to join MTech, as this would put additional burden on my preparation but I managed to convince them that I would be able to manage both). My grand father only told me that my only dream is to see you as an IAS (in villages, people still believe that there are only 2 sarkari offices who can make difference in society i.e. IAS &IPS). I kept reminding myself of the promise that I gave to my grandfather. Finally, I managed to maintain a CGPA of 8.05 in IIT and cleared UPSC exam in my first fully prepared attempt with rank of 718 and got IRS (IT) as the service. Today, when I look back on my journey, I thank my friend in college, my family members and my internal motivation to make up for the time lost by starting late helped me to clear this exam. Sometimes when I felt tired or did not want to study I sat alone in front of my mirror (which is always there on my study table, it has become a habit to study with mirror on my table because I think it helps me to concentrate) and remind myself of the challenges faced by my grandfather and father to give me such opportunities, coming from a village where we have a school till 5th class and where my friend who studied with me when I was in village (mummy and myself went to Pune where my father was posted a little later) are still doing farming, or working as truck drivers or as daily wage earners. So failure was not an option I had to succeed which kept me going.

LIST OF BOOKS

You can find this on net easily. Almost all aspirants study the same books. What makes the difference is how well you write the answers with the knowledge that you have.

Visit site mrunal.org. Read the toppers' section, at least one or two toppers with whom you are able to relate or with toppers with the optional that you want to choose. Monthly current affairs of Vision IAS is very good, almost everyone reads and insights on India is also a good website.

STUDY PLAN

There cannot be any fixed study plan. It varies for individual to individual. Some may like to start early morning, others may study late night but what is important is that you make daily goals to cover certain topics, read certain number of pages and complete them. There cannot be any fixed number of hours but a certain minimum effort has to be put consistently on daily basis.

MESSAGE TO NEWCOMERS

UPSC is a long process so first of all, mentally prepare yourself for this journey. Internal motivation is the biggest driving factor that will keep you going. Preparation must not become a burden you have to enjoy the journey. This will teach you a lot about various topics, about the society and about yourself. Choose your optional wisely (this has to be done by the individual because you have to spent most of your time with it and this is where top rankers are decided today). You can take guidance from seniors but take the final call yourself by looking at previous years' papers and your interests. Perseverance and consistency are going to be the keys to success. Keep yourself refreshed by giving yourself some free time (some game, music etc). But in the end what matters is how badly you want to succeed. And as a word of caution, don't over burden yourself by reading whatever you can lay your hand on. Plan properly. Keep reading the syllabus, follow limited sources but keep revising them.

Final words : Don't stop till you have achieved what you set out for. UPSC is just an exam, it is not a monster that one has to be afraid of. It is a beautiful exam which is a great equalizer. Students from every background gets opportunity to succeed through their dedication and efforts. Stay away from negative people, who may discourage you (Tumse Na hopayega type of people) and support of family and friend will help you at every stage.

Finally some good lines which I like although there are many but I am adding only some which I have right now.

1. Mushqil nahi hai kuch duniya main tu zara himmat to kar, khawab badlenge haqeeqat main tu zara koshish to kar.
2. (Success belongs to those who believe in the beauty of their dreams.)

❑❑

47

Name: Rahul Kumar Singh
Rank: 579, CSE-2018

Do see dreams, but do try honestly for them or else dreams are dreams will remain a dream and will always make you restless.

RAHUL KUMAR SINGH

OPTIONAL SUBJECT

Hindi

EDUCATIONAL QUALIFICATION

❖ 1. 10th - 62.5% & 12th- 76% from UP Board, Kanpur
2. B. Tech (NIT Kurukshetra) - 70%
3. MA (Geography) - 65%
4. NET JRF - Geography

PRE-SELECTION

SBI PO, Income Tax Inspector, Assistant Commissioner of Corporate Tax (UPPCS-2016)

Ideal Personality: APJ Abdul Kalam - "If You Like the Sun"

If you want to shine, first learn to meditate like the sun".

INTERESTS

Playing Badminton & table Tennis & watching movies

MAINS MARKS AND PERSONALITY TEST

Essay (Paper I): 133
General Studies- I (Paper II): 73
General Studies- II (Paper III): 94
General Studies- III (Paper IV): 80
General Studies- IV (Paper V): 94
Optional - I (Hindi) (Paper VI): 153
Optional - II (Hindi) (Paper VII): 159
Total marks in main examination: 786
Interview: 160
Total Score: 946

CIVIL SERVICE TOUR

I am very happy and it is easy for me to describe the happiness achieved on success is not. My goal from the beginning was not to go to UPSC. My goals changed over time and after taking up a job in the private sector, I felt that here financially competence is there but at the cost of social hollowness. This was the root cause that made me inspired from the narrow streets of the private sector to join the vast society. UPSC only was the medium through which I used my abilities to be able to do what I needed to do for the fulfilment of personal goals. This was the reason that in the era of pouring failures I got stronger in time. The ultimate goal is that the UPSC journey is that there is only one stop and new goals and struggles will continue in life.

Everyone has their own personal reasons for joining the civil service, so for everyone the reasons for motivation can be different in which social interactions and society. Competence to bring positive change, job diversity, job security and economic soundness etc. are included. As far as I am concerned, I have already mentioned it above.

There are many stages in UPSC and all the stages pass. Once you achieve a good rank which is a bit difficult to bring but with the right strategy and proper guidance it can be accomplished. If serious efforts are made then appropriate results should be brought in. I have been constantly changing my preparation, in the present effort, I am preparing myself for this examination for about one to one and a half years. I was satisfied about and was hopeful about success.

Since I had failed this exam many times before and it was my UPSCI had a third interview. But even in my constant realities, I always kept trying to make changes in my strategies as well as constantly. I was also trying to maintain motivation. For this, Gandhiji's strategy of struggle was also captured in his life and changing the subject. Also I took a gap of two years and stood up again with a new topic which UPSCI was also reborn in so in short, never give up, be honest with yourself, and continuing my efforts with Motivation has been the source of my success

Do not get tired, never step nor lose courage
I have seen many rounds and still the journey continues.

CONTRIBUTE TO SUCCESS

Many people directly and indirectly contribute to the success of any person is included. Many people have contributed to my success too - my parents, brother Rohit, teacher Somu and other family members as well as UPSC friend Devendra, Yogesh, and Nazmin, and office friends Vinesh and Hridesh etc. All of them continued with me in this difficult journey and inspired me constantly keep doing that you will definitely get success. I do not join any institute regularly but I have found, but for writing answers in this year's IAS mains, Vinay Sir connected and brought maturity to my writing style which directly benefited me. I would also like to thank all of the above for their contribution -

What is yours, borrowed from everyone in this life
All the iron is their only edge

OPTIONAL SUBJECT

My optional subject this year was Hindi literature. The reason for choosing this topic is my Hindi. In addition to being comfortable in the language, the subject has also been numerate and concise. The good thing about this topic is that every time you write a different and original answer to any question which has a special effect on the examiner as well as the possibility of scoring. Since my background was also through UP board-Hindi medium, there was no problem in taking it. To some extent it is true that some subjects are more pliant and easier than others. My attempt in UPSC with Geography in which I was not successful even though I was a JRF could happen. Perhaps this is also the reason that at present most of the students are getting more attracted towards some subjects and should also be because our purpose here is only UPSC.

MAIN EXAMINATION

The Big Basis of Success Outstanding Answer Writing Style

The key to success in UPSC is excellent answer writing style and hard work. Answer writing should be such that it has a positive effect on the examiner, for which the demand and nature of the question. Special attention should be paid to maps, data, charts, and contemporary references. While doing so, attention should be given to every aspect of the question. As well as writing style exercises, keeping a stop watch for as well as practicing stop writing. Continuous improvement should be made in our shortcomings. I also resolved to write an answer to Dhaka. A group was formed in the hostel with my friends Vidit and Manish and we put a stop watch used to practice writing regular answers.

My opinion is that notes should be made, but these notes should be so brief that the at the time of finals, they can be easily read before the main examination. Like optional subject just one can be included in the copy, the same should be done with GS and essay topics. And you should start making notes only when the whole subject has been read once or twice. Only then do we really know what to write in the notes and how to reduce it to be put into words. Since syllabus is very much in pre exam on which to make notes is extremely timely and not practical, so the emphasis on making notes is also mainly should be on main exam and not on pre exam.

Of course it is very useful to participate in mock test series where we are able to assess our preparation realistically, on the other hand, the main exam we can improve them by knowing about the mistakes made in it in advance.

INTERVIEW PREPARATION

I think UPSC preparations both for interview or personality development begin with. Your group is the best way to prepare for the interview which is formed during preparation and you regularly discuss various issues, become aware of the negative aspects of your personality, as well as work on it. Therefore, attention should be paid from the beginning to the UPSC. There is a reason for low selection of Hindi medium students of Hindi medium as somewhere there have also been low marks in the interview. I was a little nervous before the interview and expected it also. But since you have gone through many stages during preparation in which you. There are many ups and downs, so you would have learned to manage this stress too. I was interviewed on the board of Mr. Pradeep Kumar Joshi sir. It is believed that the marks obtained in interview from the board made a difference in my last 3 interviews respectively. If 176,160,160 marks have been scored, which would indicate the difference in the marks obtained. But if your personality is balanced and holistic in your understanding and you can easily express yourself, the board's decision will definitely have no effect on your points.

Role of online website in preparation for civil service

Surely in today's changing environment the use of websites is very much for preparation is important. There are many ace channels on YouTube that complement your preparation. Like –Onlyias, StudyIQ etc., apart from this there are many websites like - ForumIAS, DrishtiIAS that we can use regularly. But at the same time we have to also, keep in mind that everything unnecessarily distactive is bad, so unnecessary browsing of social sites should be diligently avoided.

Best time to prepare for Civil Services

The most suitable time to start preparing for civil service is simultaneously with graduation and soon after that, civil service efforts should be given, because at that time we on the one hand are most full of energy, while family and financial responsibilities are also upon us is also less. However; this is the time to start is due to your financial security and other reasons can also depend on it. I started my private job long after my graduation. While starting, I considered my strategy wrong in this matter that I have started my preparation late but one part of the strategy has always been that I always stayed connected to a job and I kept my backup, which gave me financial challenges I did not have to deal with. A minimum of one and a half to two years should be given for exam preparation and the effort should be that the preparation of all the steps should be done in parallel because all the steps are connected to each other, this will reduce the time on one side and you will you will be able to understand everything in totality.

Like I said earlier, I was regular even though I was irregular. Whenever I study lived in a mode of being completely disciplined and positive in a certain time. I used to study with energyespecially after engaging in sports activities and talking to friends.. I think any routine ideally does not change according to the person, so the candidate according to his personality make your routine as well as be disciplined, restrained, honest - first to yourself and also to those whom you have promised that you will definitely succeed.

My personal opinion is that while coming for civil service preparation. You should also think of an alternative career, because an alternative career is necessary for success. It not only protects from tensions and also provides financial security. It would be that the civil service is not the only final truth and it has a success percentage of 1% Is also less. Therefore, we should start

UPSC preparation along with graduation. So that you remain eligible for other exams as well as alternative career opportunities remain for the subject. I am also currently working as an inspector in income tax in Bhopal. I am in the office, with this I also passed JRF which was my backup plan.

Certainly, the family and academic background will have a great influence on the preparations which sometimes makes your selection too late but this background can never stop a competent candidate from getting selected in UPSC. Such candidates needs to imbibe rapid changes in themselves and accordingly mold yourself. Do not survive through new techniques and mediums but face them and keep preparing with a persistent learning approach.

I have always been inspired to think of toppers who was also one of my friends. I was selected in UPSC, so I got more positive energy from it and then go towards the new effort with full energy. My opinion still hasn't changed and I think that the readers who are reading this interview will also be towards their goals and will proceed positively and will be interviewed here next year.

This assumption is not true at all, nor is it practical to read for 16 to 18 hours. By the way, every person has different sources of success but this is my personal opinion is that, along with 7-8 hours of regular, devoted and disciplined studies, walking and sports time should also be given so that your preparation should proceed in a wholesome manner.

Since there are many stages in the civil service and many times the desired results are not achieved. It is natural to have mental tension but know the need. We have to overcome it. So I used to work on two levels, on the one hand I regularly associated with sports, which also reduced mental stress and at the same time there was also energy available for reading. On the other hand, in constant contact with such friends used to keep motivating me constantly and my stress would get ebbed away while talking to them.

Due to low selection of Hindi medium students

This year, out of a total of 759, probably only 18 have been finalized in UPSC. I have seen many reasons behind this - the first reason has been in the Hindi medium since last year. There has been a decrease in the number of students involved and at the same time one has to admit that the educational and economic status of these students are also comparatively weaker than others. They also face many challenges. Maybe that's why his personality from the very beginning, they are weaker than others, whose loss in the final interview.

They have to pay with less marks which exclude them from this race itself. This time also the number of interviewers was much higher than the final selected but the final stage due to comparatively low marks in IIT, many students were left out of the selection.

Along with this, low marks in GS is also a reason, so on GS topics also attention will have to be paid if we score even more than 0.5 marks in each paper it will be above other than. Finally, we should keep preparing keeping these aspects in mind. I would like to thank all those individuals and organizations again in my journey who stayed connected with me and constantly encouraged me, as well as reading my interview.

I sincerely thank all the readers for this and best wishes for their future and I would also like to advise that you dream, see it, but their try too sincerely or else dreams will remain dreams and you will always feel restless. Keep doing For my friends of UPSC –

What is the path, what is the way?

What is that sailor's patience test when the currents are not hostile?

❑❑

48

Name: Rajendra Chaudhary
Rank: 590, CSE-2018

The most important thing is to trust yourself. Each student's capability is different, so comparison must be avoided. Identify your weaknesses and flaws and strengthen it well.

RAJENDRA CHAUDHARY

OPTIONAL SUBJECT
Literature of Hindi Language

MEDIUM
Mains- Hindi, Interviews- English.

NATIVE PLACE
Ranigaon, Makrana Nagaur (Rajasthan)

EDUCATIONAL QUALIFICATION
- B.Tech – IIT Kharagpur (2010)
- M.A. - Hindi Literature, IGNOU (2019)

PARENTS' OCCUPATION
- **Father:** Panchayat Extension Officer
- **Mother:** Homemaker

COACHING TAKEN
- GS – Nothing
- Hindi Lit.- Kumar Sarvesh Sir (Dhyey IAS)

MARKS
- **Paper - 1:** 112
- **Paper -2:** Qualifying in Nature.

MAINS AND INTERVIEW SCORE

Essay (Paper I) - 144
General Studies- I (Paper II) - 079
General Studies- II (Paper III) - 090
General Studies- III (Paper IV) - 090
General Studies- IV (Paper V - 098
Optional - I (Hindi Litt.) (Paper VI)-157
Optional - II (Hindi Litt.) (Paper VII)- 148
Written Total- 806
Personality Test- 138
Final Total- 944

MY STRUGGLE

When I started preparing in 2013, I was 26-27 years, that is, the age at which the rest of the people get three years of service, then I started at that time, which simply meant that I was mentally prepared for the ups and downs. I never had any doubt about the appointment because from a rural background, I had travelled to IIT and then to Japan, when I was so confident in overcoming these tasks. I was quite sure that if I make solid and serious efforts, I will definitely get success.

But today if you analyze the previous journey in 2019, you will know that many things did not happen according to my anticipation. When I started the journey, I had set a goal of just 2 years in front of me. Luckily in the very first attempt, I got an opportunity to reach the interview and things according to the criteria but after attending the interview three more times, I was still selected in the final list. If it could not happen, then life was filled with ups and downs.

During this time I used to remember the same sentence again and again, "Rajendra you are the first generation of your family those who are trying to overcome such a big hurdle at the national level will definitely face problems". One option to avoid this was to leave and go to the private sector for a high-package job. But I preferred to stay strong, because I knew that UPSC was like a marathon race or boxing, in which if you dare to fall and win, you can win the match. After 6 whole years, the struggle was successful.

Changing my strategy over time was also another thing that challenged me in this difficult and precious time. After first 2 attempts with geography, I felt that the optional subject is keeping me out of the final list, so I decided to change it and took 'Hindi literature', which proved to be a right decision.

Before I started preparing for IAS, I was a teacher and I used to talk to my students. I used to teach them, so they contributed a lot to my success. Apart from these, once in childhood, my father wrote me a letter and told me that I have the ability to become an IAS. It is important, whenever I had got inferiority complex, this thing used to give me courage. Then on the other side in this struggle. My mother, sister and wife joined me, which made the way much easier. After the 2016 mains, I started a job in the Customs Department and got the full support of my colleagues and officers there.

At the end, I would like to tell you that some of your habits, favorite things will definitely uplift you. Many times under stress I used to go to the shelter of kaju katli, a favourite sweet made from cashew. I partake and fill myself with its sweetness and would start preparing for the exam with renewed enthusiasm.

Message for candidates

- ❖ Most important, trust in yourself. Every student is different, so compare yourself should be avoided with anyone. Identify your weaknesses and strengths and strategize.
- ❖ In this exam, one should neither listen nor listen to anyone, just by looking at the rank, because sometimes someone's success does not teach us as much as someone's failure.
- ❖ This essay requires different strategies for essay, GS 1, 2,3, 4 and optional subject, which does not necessarily get you in one of the successful / unsuccessful candidates. So pay attention to more toppers (successful) than you and accept and reject things according to your abilities.
- ❖ This whole test is like a 'black box', in which no one knows what exactly happening, so keep the most trust in yourself and keep your mind in everything because UPSC does not want stereotypes. 'Notification' should be read very well because it is the only thing in which the UPSC tells how it needs an officer.
- ❖ Must study in a group, i.e., you should have a close group of 3-4 friends because there is power in the organization. I have seen many groups being appointed together in my preparation, my group is also an example of this.
- ❖ There is nothing better than your notes, you can refer to the notes of many people, as much as you can read. But the final notes should be on your own and should be rehearsed as much as possible.
- ❖ 2-3 Always keep in touch with elected people so that when there is a problem you can talk to them. They can be from your area, you can be from college, they can be relatives. Or there may be acquaintances whose 'alternative' subject is the same, which is your subject.
- ❖ Nothing is impossible, even word impossible itself says, I am possible.

List of books

I had only one effort, instead of a new book every time, one book should be read many times, provided it. The book should cover the entire curriculum in itself and did nothing special for this.

My partners were:

1. mrunal.org - List of books for all subjects is given.
2. Youtube- ONLYIAS channel
3. 'The Hindu'- Editorial
4. Vision - Current Affairs (Current Affairs)
5. Insightonindia - Current Affairs (Current Affairs)

The benefit of the above will be fruitful, only if you include them in your notes.

❑❑

49

Name: Krishan Kumar Poonia
Rank: 632, CSE-2018

"Failures are conspicuous at different stages of this exam for most of us. Therefore, a detailed self-analysis of failure must be done so that failure doesn't get repeated again and keep working hard and never lose confidence & hope. Sure, you will get success in civil services."

KRISHAN KUMAR POONIA

OPTIONAL SUBJECT
Public Administration

MEDIUM
English

NATIVE PLACE
Bansur, Alwar (Rajasthan)

EDUCATIONAL QUALIFICATION
- B.E. Computer Technology
- M.A. Public Administration
- NET-JRF

PARENTS' OCCUPATION
- **Father:** Farmer
- **Mother:** Home Maker

COACHING TAKEN
- GS -Vajiram& Ravi
- Optional- Mohanti sir

MARKS
- **Paper - 1:** 115
- **Paper -2:** 105

MAINS AND INTERVIEW SCORE
Essay (Paper I) - 094
General Studies- I (Paper II) - 083
General Studies- II (Paper III) - 108
General Studies- III (Paper IV) - 100
General Studies- IV (Paper V) - 096
Optional - I (Pub. Ad.) (Paper VI)-144
Optional - II (Pub. Ad.) (Paper VII)- 149
Written Total- 774
Personality Test- 165
Final Total- 939

MY JOURNEY

(a) How to motivate oneself and overcome failure

- Th journey of civil services has its own challenges. First of all, one should accept that fact that it will not me as smooth as we planned for most of the aspirants. There will be ups and downs. In such situations support of family members and close friends will be instrumental. I stayed away from distractions of social media and whats app and stayed in touch with only few friends who inspired me. I also appeared and selected for several other exams like CAPF Assistant Commandant, RAS, IB etc. This motivated me to do more and put extra efforts.
- Failures are conspicuous at different stages of this exam for most of us. Therefore, a detailed self-analysis of failure must be done so that failure doesn't get repeated again and keep working hard and never lose confidence & hope.

(b) Booklist and study material

- In general, I followed, booklist given on mrunal.org website.
- GS 1- Nitin Singhania's notes for art and culture, Periyar's Indian geography, Ram Ahuja for society
- GS 2 -Newspaper and Lok Sabha Rajyasabha written questions.
- GS 3- Yojana, and Mrunalvideos and articles, PIB features
- GS 4 - Atul Garg Sir's notes.

SUGGESTIONS FOR NEWCOMERS

- There is no dearth of information regarding Civil Services preparation in this digital world. One should not follow toppers' strategy blindly but try to develop your own strategy which will work for you.
- Essay, ethics and optional are the important aspects of this exam. I ignored essay and marks are reflection of that. Therefore, give sufficient time to essay preparation too.
- Identify your weak areas and put extra efforts in it.
- Rather than reading from multiple sources one should make a single source as base and then improve it with other sources and revising it multiple times. This really helped me in public administration.
- A small group of dedicated aspirants for peer review, discussion and notes sharing can be really helpful.

❑❑

50

Name: Mintu Lal Meena
Rank: 664, CSE-2018

Continued hard work in the right direction for success in the Civil Services Examination, positive thinking, patience and confidence are very important. Work hard in the right direction continuously. You will surely succeed.

MINTU LAL MEENA

OPTIONAL SUBJECT
History

MEDIUM
Hindi

NATIVE PLACE
Village-Dharanwas, Post-Paparda, District- Dausa

EDUCATIONAL QUALIFICATION
- B.A. (Non Collegiate) History, Economics, political Science M.A. (Non Collegiate) Modern History of India

PARENTS' OCCUPATION
- **Father:** Agriculture
- **Mother:** Homemaker

COACHING TAKEN
- Drishti IAS (G.S. , Optional and Essay)

MAINS MARKS AND PERSONALITY TEST
Essay (Paper I): 124
General Studies- I (Paper II): 069
General Studies- II (Paper III): 094
General Studies- III (Paper IV): 086
General Studies- IV (Paper V): 095
Optional - I (History) (Paper VI): 153
Optional - II (History) (Paper VII): 149
Written Total: 770
Personality Test: 160
Final Total: 930

MY JOURNEY

My family is dependent on agriculture. After 12th standard, due to poor financial condition of the family, I had to take up a job and I became Patwari (since 9 January 2014). After graduation, I got a job and moved to Delhi for preparation (since July 2016).

Since it costs a lot to live in Delhi, I needed my friends Mahesh Kumar Rajni Meena (husband and wife and Patwari) contributed. This success would have been impossible without their support and inspiration. Earlier in 2012, I got admission in NIT, Calicut through AIEEE but due to personal reasons I left the institute and did B.A. instead started preparing for civil service.

I reached the interview in my first attempt but could not get selected finally. In 2018, with my second attempt I got 669 rank. I am likely to receive IRS-IT service.

MESSAGE FOR NEWCOMERS

- My message to the new candidates who start preparing for the civil service is that they are in the civil service Understand nature, analyze previous year question papers and start preparing accordingly.
- Limit the source of your study and revise them frequently so that you have a strong grip on the subject.
- Mock test for preliminary examination and focus on current affairs.
- Write more practice test series to get better marks in mains exam.
- Prepare your own resume better during interviews and group yourself with some friends, Create and mock interviews with each other. Its benefits are available. Being abreast with information about current fffairs for all three phases is a must.
- Continued hard work, positive thinking, patience in the right direction for success in Civil Services ExaminationAnd confidence is very important. Work hard in the right direction continuously. You will definitely get success.
- Stress is natural during preparation. For this, your parents, guides or good friends talk to, give time to your hobbies. Always stay away from negative people and negative thoughts.

❑❑

51

Name: Sachin Kumar
Rank: 669, CSE-2018

"No goal is big, one who wins is not scared"

SACHIN KUMAR

OPTIONAL SUBJECT
History
MEDIUM
Hindi
NATIVE PLACE
Born Meerut, later shifted to Aligarh
EDUCATIONAL QUALIFICATION
MA (History)
SV College, Aligarh.
UGC NET (2009, 2013, History)
PRE-SELECTION
Assistant Commandant, 2012 BSF,
Lower PCS 2009 (UP),
Commercial Tax Officer (2012 batch,
2014 to present working)
PARENTS' OCCUPATION

- **Father:** Late Shri Veeri Singh, was a soldier in UP Police
- **Mother:** Sunflower, Housewife

MARKS
Prelims: Paper -1: 89.34 and Paper -2: 77
Mains: 928
MAINS MARKS AND PERSONALITY TEST
Essay (Paper I): 146
General Studies- I (Paper II): 82
General Studies- II (Paper III): 88
General Studies- III (Paper IV): 80
General Studies- IV (Paper V): 83
Optional - I (History) (Paper VI): 149
Optional - II (History) (Paper VII): 151
Interview: 149

NO GOAL IS BIG, ONE WHO WINS IS NOT SCARED

Those lines never let me down. My own decision to pursue civil service which I determined after the death of my father in the encounter. Ever a pressure on me, no longer Yes! During my studies, I got to hear the words of my neighbors, which was negative. This selection was the 6th attempt. Could not pass prelims exam in first 3 attempts.

The reason for the trend towards civil service was the crisis I had over my family. When my mother and brother, it took me 6 years for pension, and this work was done by DM Aligarh in just 2 days. Doing it was really motivating for me. However, I was also disappointed during the exam. In this hour, my brother Rajendra Kumar, sister-in-law, mother-in-law, sisters-in-law, wife Preeti, Guru Manoj Chauhan, friend Manoj Kumar gave me a huge positive support.

During preparation I did not take any coaching support for GS though VISION IASCurrent day 15 days class, test series of optional subjects in construction IAS, Reunion and I took a series of coaching in Ethics.

CANDIDATES TIPS

- Regular study of daily newspapers, I Dainik Jagran, and THE HINDU Make notes of ONLY IAS YOU TUBE
- Planning, Regular Study of Chronicle Magazine.
- Geography: NCERT and Examination Voice (India and World)
- Polity: Laxmikant, Bare Act optional subject

Notes of IGNOU

Jha Shrimali (Ancient India), Harish Chandra Verma (Medieval)

Modern India-Grover, Spectrum, Bipin Chandra

* For the exam, I think that before the exam, you should prepare with the diagram at home. DJSA writing regularly for time management.

❑❑

52

Name: Dinesh Kumar Meena
Rank: 678, CSE-2018

"Every person is born with talent. You only need to find your talent and prove it with something unexpected."

DINESH KUMAR MEENA

OPTIONAL SUBJECT
Electrical Engineering

MEDIUM
English

NATIVE PLACE
Karauli (Rajasthan)

EDUCATIONAL QUALIFICATION
- B.Tech – IIT Bombay (2016)

PARENTS' OCCUPATION
- **Father:** Govt Employee (Indian Railways)
- **Mother:** Homemaker

COACHING TAKEN
- GS – Vajiram, Optional - crash course nextias (3 month)

MARKS
Prelims: Paper – 1: 99 and **Paper -2: 112**

MAINS AND INTERVIEW SCORE
765 plus interview 160
Optional 255

CONTACT

fb: https://www.facebook.com/dinesh.goyadi
https://www.instagram.com/dinesh.goyadi/
https://twitter.com/dineshgoyadi

MY JOURNEY

(a) Struggle

- Started my prep in June 2016 when I joined Vajiram. Before that, I had not prepared for Civils in my college. So I started afresh. Luckily, I had my brother who was preparing for Civils to guide me. I took (Political Science and International Relations) as my optional subject as I didn't want to opt for 'Engineering' optional.

- I was able to clear my 1st prelims on 18th June, 2017 as I prepared extensively in last 2 months of prelims. Also polity was dominating subject in 2017 prelims and I had good grasp of the subject. I also cleared my 2017 mains but my paper didn't go well as I had not taken mains test series seriously. But the saddest thing that happened to me was my interview. I got a score of 116 out of 275, which was among the lowest scores ever awarded. I missed the cutoff by 4 marks. Now only 1 month was left for next prelims, which was on 3rd June. With the baggage of failure, I studied very hard during this month and by God's grace, I was able to clear my 2nd prelims. Now rewinding back a bit and talking about the blunder I did. I changed my optional to Electrical Engineering. If you ask me why I did that, my answer would be I don't know! So I started preparing for Electrical. I haven't had good history with Electrical. Soon after reading for few days, I realised the syllabus is huge and its very difficult to cover it in 3 months after which I had to give my mains. So I joined optional advance course. I found it very helpful as I had zero knowledge of Electrical. I gave more than 80 percent of time to my optional and very little for GS because I was not even confident of scoring 200 marks in optional. I did not joined any GS test series either. 3 months passed I completed what could. I cleared it again. I had an idea that I would clear it though my marks wouldn't be as good as my previous attempt. Now comes the interview. This time I got Manoj Joshi's board, very cordial. I did average and got what I expected (160 marks). When the final result came, I was hopeful of getting my name in the list. Though I was sure I would not get through IAS, as my paper didn't go well but the feeling of getting selected was amazing as I had already seen failure in my 1st attempt. But sadly, this was not the end, appearing again in 2019 prelims, will be my 3rd attempt. Hopefully will write this again next year.

(b) List of Books

- The trinity of Laxmikant, Shankar IAS and spectrum for Polity environment and history. If you are not taking any coaching I will suggest go through mrunal courses (all economy, culture, geograhy etc). If you are joining Vajiram then you can just watch culture mrunal videos rather reading Nitin Singhania. Also geography from NCERT is important. Beside that part 365 and mains 365 for current affairs. If you don't understand these books you can read any book you want to develop your aptitude to understand these. You can include NCERT's, other coaching material etc.

MESSAGE FOR NEW COMERS

- For prelims- understand the evolving pattern, now the old ways of rigorous studying and mugging won't work. Its both good and bad thing. You can clear the prelims without studying much and may not clear after lots of hard work. So my tip is focus more on newspaper. Complete your basic books as soon as possible so that you can give enough time to newspapers. Understand concepts rather than just having an idea. Focus more on technological aspects (digital, space, AI etc). Also dont just read one newspaper, also be active online and have an idea about other important news through magazines, other newspapers etc. And finally the importance of test series. Now the paper is such that you cannot perfectly know answers to many questions. So much will depend on logical guesses and intuitions. So, you will have to prepare your mind to have that intuition aligned with UPSC. So give tests very seriously and build your experience....
- For mains— choose your optional wisely, syllabus, last year's papers and even read it for few days before choosing your optional. Talk with someone who has given mains with same optional subject.
- Test series for mains is also very important. At first you will be able to do 15 ques max, but with practice you will be able to attempt all. So give as many tests as possible. Check topper's answer sheets to have idea about how to write.
- Finally, for interview, the only advice I will give you is be confident and say 'no' if you don't know answer to very basic questions even as basic as who is the president of India. Dont feel guilty or ashamed. The way you answer matter more than what you answer.

❑❑

53

Name: Hemant Singh
Rank: 679, CSE 2018

"Do not try to compare yourself with others. You will ultimately do things in your own unique way and comparison with anyone else might not help in your development."

HEMANT SINGH

OPTIONAL SUBJECT
Philosophy

MEDIUM
English

EDUCATION QUALIFICATION
- B.Tech- IIT Bombay (2012)

PARENTS' OCCUPATION
- **Father:** RAS (Retired)
- **Mother:** Homemaker

COACHING TAKEN
- GS- Khan Study Group, Philosophy - Mitras IAS

MAINS AND INTERVIEW SCORE
Essay (Paper I) - 127
General Studies- I (Paper II) - 082
General Studies- II (Paper III) - 083
General Studies- III (Paper IV) - 085
General Studies- IV (Paper V) - 097
Optional - I (Philosophy) (Paper VI)-143
Optional - II (Philosophy) (Paper VII)- 143
Written Total- 760
Personality Test- 165
Final Total- 925

MY JOURNEY

(a) About myself

- True inspiration behind pursuing Civil Services were my parents. It was their commitment and sacrifices which finally helped me to achieve this. Family support is extremely important in this journey.
- I was from Engineering background but I chose Philosophy as my optional subject. My score in previous attempts was very low in philosophy. I chose to continue with same optional even after failing many times. So having faith in the subject and working on your own weaknessess is really important.
- I used to get distracted very easily whether it is spending time with friends or social media etc. All these distractions really cost much in the long run. In competitive exams like Civil Services, difference of very few marks can lead to selection or rejection. Therefore, I tried to minimize my distractions as much as possible.
- Lastly, I never doubted myself in this whole journey. I knew one day, I will clear it and that belief kept me going even during tough times. So strong self belief is must for a long journey like Civil Services.

(b) How to overcome ups/downs

- Anyone can't remain motivated all the times. Mood swings among aspirants is a common thing. One should understand that we must keep our mid fresh and calm all the time. One can take short breaks or long breaks to refresh.
- Talking with friends and family regularly also helps in keeping the morale high.
- Don't read a subject continously for long hours. We should read multiple subjects in a day so that the interest remains.
- Don't try to worry about things which are out of your control. It is difficult to do but one needs to learn how to focus on the given task inspite of several external issues. This quality will also be needed during the work as a civil servant.
- Develop a hobby and try to save some time everyday for your hobby.It can be as simple as listening to music.

- Don't try to compare yourself with others. You will ultimately do things in your own unique way and comparison with anyone else might not help in your development.

MESSAGE FOR NEWCOMERS

- Organise your preparation and study material from 1st day itself. Have a time table and try to stick to it as much as you can.
- Choose your optional wisely. You have to really score well in your chosen subject and if the subject is not interesting enough for you, it will be difficult to clear the exam.
- Practise as many mock tests as possible for both prelims and mains.
- Study consistently. Don't lose time in doing irrelevant things during the course of preparation.
- Start enjoying the process and stop worrying about the outcome. You must become more learned and wise person because of this preparation and this wisdom gained will remain with you forever.
- Read newspaper daily.

❑❑

54

Name: Pawan Kumar Meena
Rank: AIR-702, CSE-2018

"Never fight war on two fronts (Germany lost 2nd World War), put all your efforts on UPSC front only."

PAWAN KUMAR MEENA

OPTIONAL SUBJECT
Economics

MEDIUM
English

EDUCATION QUALIFICATION
❖ IIT kharagpur (2017 batch)

COACHING TAKEN
❖ GS Coach Taken : Vajiram and Ravi

MARKS
Prelims: Gs paper: 101 **Paper 2:** 114

MAINS AND INTERVIEW SCORE

Essay (Paper I) - 107
General Studies- I (Paper II) - 089
General Studies- II (Paper III - 107
General Studies- III (Paper IV) - 101
General Studies- IV (Paper V) - 092
Optional - I (Economics) (Paper VI)-143
Optional - II (Economics) (Paper VII) - 123
Written Total- 762
Personality Test- 157
Final Total- 919

MY JOURNEY

(a) How to overcome ups/downs

- Civil service exam process is very lengthy and hence it gave me ample opportunity to think about quitting in between. It's natural if you feel every other day about failure during your preparation phase.
- If you feel low or stranded while preparing seriously, it symbolizes that you are in right direction so keep moving.
- I can summarise this exam process in three levels as follows:

  Prelims: In this round, more than academic you feel social pressure.

  Mains: At this level, you feel self pressure as you, yourself get to know a whole lot about yourself.

  Interview: In this round, you face expectation's pressure.
- To deal with low phase, pursue your hobbies, talk to your parents and with few selected close friends.
- Don't overburden yourself and try to implement good habits in gradual manner as discipline is essential for your upcoming life. Try to face your fear instead of evading it, for example, if you fear answer writing, write it.

  Be positive and no need to compare yourself with previous toppers, it's perfectly fine if you score very low, what matters in the long run is your growth rate, so try to improve day by day.

MESSAGE FOR NEW COMERS

- Firstly, prepare yourself mentally for 2-3 years' devotion to this single cause and also try to answer, why you want to pursue civil services.
- Download the syllabus and purchase NCERTs (6-12). Build your foundation and try to learn the art of expressing things simply effectively.
- Be selective with study material and follow 1-2 standard books. I would suggest if possible, get hands on Vajiram and Ravi GS coaching material and 1 standard book for every subject. Then make your own consolidated notes keeping in mind UPSC syllabus.

- Please make sure that whatever sources you follow, bring them all to one concise notes form without organizing things you only increase your number of attempts.
- Make a year long plan for GS and optional subject. Give at least 4 months for Prelims in your first attempt.
- Eat healthy and live in stress free positive environment.

Additional

Never fight war on two fronts (Germany lost WW2), put all your efforts on UPSC front only.

Use Google feed (personalized) for Technology, Agriculture and Economics related news.

❑❑

55

Name: Devendra Prakash Meena
Rank: 705

"Never bring to your mind the idea that I will not be appointed, because the subconscious, The mind also has a very important contribution. If your subconscious mind If you constantly inspire, you will definitely get success.

DEVENDRA PRAKASH MEENA

OPTIONAL SUBJECT
Hindi literature
MEDIUM
Hindi
NATIVE PLACE
Kolvagram (Dausa)
EDUCATIONAL QUALIFICATION
❖ B.Tech (Mechanical Engineering) IIT Guwahati
12th (83.38%) RBSE
10th (90.17%) RBSE
PARENTS' OCCUPATION
❖ **Father:** Teacher
❖ **Mother:** Housewife
COACHING TAKEN
Took admission in a renowned coaching institute of Delhi on 3-4
After months of realization, she left in the middle.
MARKS
Prelims: Paper -1: 91.34 and Paper -2: 108.33
MAINS MARKS AND PERSONALITY TEST
Essay (Paper I): 135
General Studies- I (Paper II): 084
General Studies- II (Paper III): 094
General Studies- III (Paper IV): 082
General Studies- IV (Paper V): 086
Optional - I (Hindi Litt.) (Paper VI): 154
Optional - II (Hindi Litt.) (Paper VII): 144
Written Total: 779
Personality Test: 140
Final Total: 919
Instagram - *dpmeena94*

MY TRIP

(A) My struggle

I belong to a place in Dausa district where someone in the vicinity of this service doesn't even think about. In such a situation, preparation of civil service had to be started without any guidance. The first problem was what medium to choose. Taught in Hindi till 12th and in English at IIT. Then, keeping his interest ahead, he chose Hindi medium. The second problem was due to the language medium being Hindi, a mechanical subject could not be allowed. Someone advised that B.Tech people should take geography, so took I it without thinking. 24 in first attempt could not pass the main examination by marks, due to geography. I secured only 203 marks. Then instead of seeking advice from someone else, I preferred my own interest and Hindi literature for the second attempt. I had no one to guide me about the choice of subject and language medium should be taken or correct by mistake.

My advice to the candidates who start preparing is just that -

- See the medium by looking at yourself, not by looking at someone else.
- Take optional subjects also according to your own interest.
- Until you strengthen your mind, you will not get success, first of all strengthen your mind

Do it is difficult to succeed in this exam but not impossible.

Only those who keep the faith will be able to move forward.

(B) Study Plan

My school teacher once said that it is better to read a book ten times than read ten books once. This is the strategy, I used while preparing for the Civil Services Examination.

Timely and frequent rehearsal is an important point of civil service exam preparation. As the date of the exam approaches, rehearsal becomes very important.

The practice of writing answers for the main examination should be done along with starting the preparation. Otherwise this work will go backward.

I would like to offer some advice for prelims to clear all optional subjects. It is not necessary to have the correct answers. It is more important to find the wrong option. At present, the paper is coming in this pattern. Instead of the test series of the coaching institute, UPSC paper of past 5-6 years is more important to know at which level UPSC thinks.

List of books

- NCERT 9th to 12th (History, Geography, Political Science), 9th-10th Science, 11th12th Economics
- History of modern India - any spectrum from ancient times to middle ages Coaching Notes (I read the 'vision' notes)
- Political Science - M. Laxmikant
- Economy - mainly current news
- Book of Environment - Vision
- Indian Society - NCERT of 11th 12th

Newspaper - Dainik Jagran

Hindi literature - I got only 3 months for preparation, then I only have notes of vision and read test series.

MESSAGE FOR CANDIDATES

How to handle the problems faced before and during the preparation of this exam and in relation to what the strategy should be, I want to tell you a few things -

1. Before preparation

The biggest misconception regarding this exam is that for this only intelligent people from childhood can pass. So I want to tell you that there is nothing like the day you started preparing, that if you study in the right direction from the same day, then to pass the exam in one and a half years will be in position You just have to be confident in yourself.

Someone around you prepared for 3-4 years and if they were not selected, most people start to underestimate themselves. Everyone's thinking and reading attitude is different, If this happens then stay away from such people and their advice which will discourage you.

One big problem that new students face is whether to take coaching or not, would it be right to go to Delhi or not? So for this I want to share my experience. For GS here is no need for coaching. Get more information in less time by reading by yourself. Coaching of optional subject can be taken because for this a little in depth reading does matter. It is not even necessary to go to Delhi. The only benefit of going to Delhi seems that there is an environment conducive to civil service examinations. There is no compulsion that you have to go to Delhi to pass. If your home's financial status supports coaching, if you are getting compelled, then start preparing from home without getting upset.

2. During preparation

During preparation, the candidates make many types of mistakes. I read only for the prelims then after that I will study for the main exam. My advice is that the nature of this exam is such that you cannot take prelims and mains separately. Your Success Stories of IAS Exam Crackers 195, the preparation of both will have to be taken together. 2 months before the prelims even if only the prelims must read. The second mistake I made is that I will start writing the answer only after the preparation is complete. My advices is that answer writing should start from day one because answer writing is an art that slowly develops do not come in a day. Hence the practice of writing something must be started early.

The third mistake is by ignoring the essay. While the essay plays a pivotal roles. So essay writing should also be practiced once or twice a month.

The fourth mistake is when they compare themselves to each other. He read this book and I did this, it is better to read a book well than to run after ten books. For example, 'Spectrum' is sufficient for history, so why waste time reading Vipin Chandra.

The fifth mistake is not to read the newspaper. While reading the newspaper it is more important than reading the books, because what you have read from it is a rehearsal and mutual affiliation of subjects. The current pattern of the exam is similar to this. Reading newspaper 4-5 hours is too much. Most universally forbidden.

The sixth mistake is to evaluate yourself from the test series of coaching institutes. Test series is for practice only. Avoid being discouraged by making them the basis of your evaluation. Analyze UPSC's 10-year questions instead of how UPSC thinks, that would be more effective.

At the end I would like to say that never bring the idea that puts you in condition of disappointment, because the subconscious mind also has a very important contribution. If your subconscious mind continuously encourage you, you will definitely get success. Medium and optional subject should be as per your choice, not to see anyone in this field.

❑❑

56

Name: Vijendra Kumar Meena
Rank: 707, CSE-2018

Life without struggle is also of no use, so do not be afraid of challenges, compete with them, you will surely get success.

VIJENDRA KUMAR MEENA

OPTIONAL SUBJECT
History

MEDIUM
Hindi

NATIVE PLACE
Bamanwas, Sawai Madhopur, Rajasthan

EDUCATIONAL QUALIFICATION
❖ BA + MA, (class 10th class failed)

PARENTS' OCCUPATION
❖ **Father:** Agriculture
❖ **Mother:** Homemaker

COACHING TAKEN OR SELF STUDY
आरंभ में मैं कोचिंग ली लेकिन स्वाध्याय का कोई विकल्प नहीं होता

MARKS
Prelims: Paper -1: 120.00 and Paper -2: 121.68

MAINS MARKS AND PERSONALITY TEST
Essay (Paper I): 121
General Studies- I (Paper II): 085
General Studies- II (Paper III): 090
General Studies- III (Paper IV): 071
General Studies- IV (Paper V): 089
Optional - (History) (Paper VI): 152
Optional - (History) (Paper VII): 154
Written Total: 762 ❖ Personality Test: 157
Final Total: 919

LIST OF BOOKS / STUDY MATERIALS
1. NCERT books for basic study
2. Daily newspaper
3. Online material-only (iasinsightias-4) govt. reports ex. NITI Aayog, ARC Report etc.

MY JOURNEY

Initially due to the rural environment, my family did not allow for preparation because my family had economic issues. So I initially prioritized my job and first attempted in 2015. The main exam was conducted with the job of bank clerk and the interview stopped at number eight after which I quit the job and the second attempt was positive about success in 2016 but low marks in English did not get success. Some mistakes reduced my marks in prelims exam hall in 2017 and could not clear off which had to be changed due to lack of confidence in the answer to 6 questions and 5 questions went wrong! Now there was severe disappointment in life as well as due to drought in agriculture. Family pressure also started to be felt. Due to which I had to take up the job of Goods Guard in Railways. During the railway training, my friend was selected in the civil service. This again infused confidence in me for success. While thinking of not appearing in civil exams in 2018 through continued persistence in the fourth attempt, I finally achieved with 707 rank, in which I took history as optional subject and got 306 marks in Hindi, but low score in General Studies gave Hindi Medium a good rank. The cooperation of my friend Shashikant in this success was amazing, whose number 306 in history. But the final selection could not be made.

(A) Suggestions for Prelims

- Take test series (insightas / vision) coaching, along with NCERT Base books
- Be constantly aware of the current news of newspapers as well as any coaching.
- Write two to three times

(B) Scheme for GS

- Test series are extremely important for civil services.
- Make notes on some topics of General Studies 1, 2, 3, Ex. Poverty, Education, Agriculture, Rural development, Women Empowerment etc.
- Use point wise answer, mapping, diagram etc. in main examination
- Focus more attention on essays and ethics as well as optional papers

- Optional subject history-NCERT basic books class notes + test series specially focus mapping part According to me the material should be limited. 3-4 Practice the bar.

Interview

- Occasional with optional subjects and educational, family etc. background. Prepare it well.
- Give mock interview 5-6
- In front of the interview board - Be restrained and calm as the board is very supportive.

MESSAGE FOR CANDIDATES

- Success and failure are the integral part of life but be optimistic, continuity and hard work is necessary and there is no alternative to hardwork.
- Make English medium a priority.
- Choose the optional subject thoughtfully.
- Focus on guidance, strategy and smart work.
- Focus and keep study material limited.
- Prepare all the three phases of the exam simultaneously and not separately because the present mode of examination is changing. Keep the source of study material limited.

❑❑

57

Name: Satender Singh
Rank: 714, CSE-2018

All that matters for this exam is self belief, love for oneself, equanimity and consistency, and most of all, revision, revision and revision.

SATENDER SINGH

OPTIONAL SUBJECT
Political Science

MEDIUM
English

NATIVE PLACE
Amroha district, Uttar Pradesh

EDUCATIONAL QUALIFICATION
- M.A. Political Science & Int. Relation from JNU, Delhi

PARENTS' OCCUPATION
- **Father:** Farmer
- **Mother:** House wife

COACHING TAKEN
No

MAINS MARKS AND PERSONALITY TEST
Mains examination: 744
Optional - (Political science): 260
Written Total: 744
Personality Test: 173
Final Total: 917

MY JOURNEY IN BRIEF

I was born in Amroha district of remote rural Uttar Pradesh to a farmer family. When I was 1 and a half year old, I got a wrong injection in pneumonia which damaged my optical nerves resulting in me permanently losing my eyesight. As a child, I'd constantly strive to outsmart the children of my age, and would try to beat them In their own games. I'd constantly explore the alternative strategies to lessen the effect of my blindness and to use myself more effectively to outsmart them. I had an energy simmering inside me, I wanted to read and write just like them, so, I'l listen to them reciting alphabets, or mathematical tables and would memorise them even before they could. And I'd derive pleasure out of the fact that I was smarter than them. It was a comforting cushion. We'd constantly devise mechanism and reinvent the games so that my disability does not come on the way. The children who'd be playing racing, or Kabaddi, would make me their manager, so that I could listen to and solve any dispute. Similar accommodations were widespread in my childhood. I wanted to play cricket, and we had a plastic ball, but the ball was bouncy on a harder surface and I couldn't hit it because I couldn't see it. My friends came up with a strategy. We, took out the small cycle paddle balls and put them in to the ball. The ball started making sounds and I could listen to the sound and hit the ball very effectively. This all drove me to believe that children are more accommodative and inclusive in comparison to the grown ups. The grownups whine and grown about efficiency, productivity and all that in the name of inclusion and accommodation for a person with disability. The reality is, they don't want to change their old learned ways of working. But the children are very flexible. And hence, children can be more innovative, inventive, accommodative and inclusive than any grown up.

My parents were anxious about my education. My mother never got an opportunity to read and write and my father just read may be till class 5. They had no idea how a visually challenged kid could learn. But they'd consistently think about engraving the alphabets on a hard paper and make me touch them and identify them. one fine day,one of my uncles, who works in delhi, was travling in a DTC bus. He saw a blind student who was wearing a watch in his hand, was touching the hands of the watch and telling time. He was pleasantly surprised, and inquired all about him. Hence he discovered the school for blind kids. They could use Braille, mathematical taylor frame and other such devices and could easily read and write. They could use screen reading softwares, or voice over mechanisms and could understand by listening. They could harness the technology and compete with the kids in other schools effectively. My school taught me self dependence self belief and the fact that nothing is impossible. I used Braille, and then computer, by ssing screen reading softwares, listening to audio recorded books and e books on the computer.

Sometimes I turn back and think, the smallest of events, the tinniest of incidents in our life, has a profound value. Had that blind student not being wearing the Braille watch that day, my uncle wouldn't even have noticed him, and I'd still be a 27 year old blind farmer, who always wanted to outsmart my counterparts. That single event of that guy seeing time by touching the watch changed my life forever.

My school was a Hindi medium school. And those of us who were aspiring for bigger things, always idealized St. Stephens college. We heard it was the best one can have in India. I wanted to get in to it by the time I was in 12th standard. I did get good Marks. The interview went well, and I did get selected in to that institution. And a new journey began.

The college was very English. And I knew very little of it. There were students from all over the globe, so they'd speak in multiple accents which was puzzling for me. By the time I'd figure out the meaning of one sentence, my teacher would say five more, and I'd be left lost. But I wanted to try. I'd try speaking in English. And I could sense people making faces. Some of them even mocked me. It did hurt, but it propelled me to learn even harder. My friends suggested I drop out of the institution to pursue my graduation elsewhere with hindi medium. But I wanted to continue. I downloaded the ncert books from third class onwards, which I already had read in hindi, and I started reading them in English. I could see my fellow scholars not understanging or appreciating its value and relevance. But I did it. And by the time I reached to 11th standard history, I could see what was going on in class. I could form answers, and teachers were appreciative. They encouraged and supported me like they'd support their own child. Majority of the students were accommodative and appreciative. The college as a whole embraced me, accepted as I was and fundamentally brought in profound positive transformations in me.

I came to Jawaharlal Nehru university for my masters in politics and international relations. I did fairly good here. And was considered one of the budding scholars for higher studies. I always wanted to be a professor. That life style of reading, introspecting, reflecting and stimulating fellow minds always fascinated me. I idealized the personality of a professor. I went on to do my M.phil on the role of emotions in international politics. And then enrolled in P.hd on the theme sovereignty in cyberspace.

Since I always wanted to be a professor, I did get an opportunity. A vacancy for Ad-hoc assistant professor came out in Sri Aurobindo college evening in 2015. I appeared and got selected in the interview.i've been teaching since august 3, 2015. Teaching like always a wonderful experience, very stimulating, very calming, I derive so much of spiritual satisfaction out of teaching.

But I realized something was amiss. I wanted to have a wider and deeper recognition for myself. I wanted to be recognized as someone who could change the things, create a meaningful difference. As someone who despite disability can accomplish whatever they want. Moreover, I could see lots of stereotypes, prejudices and lots of biases prevailing against the people with disability. And I wanted to prove the people wrong.

I thought I can be more useful and more effective in civil services. Hence I took a the first attempt in 2016. I didn't take that exam seriously, and it didn't take me seriously.

I reppeared in 2017, and as I was gearing up for mains, I developed intestinal infection. I was admitted in hospitals for around 3 days around September 15th. It s spoiled almost a month and I missed the interview call by 9 marks.

2018, things went all right, and I got rank 714.

I now believe I could have got a better rank. But since I was doing my Phd. Was teaching and then was preparing for upsc, it did take a toll on the rank. I'd advise the fellow aspirants not to ride in multiple boats at a time. If you want to do UPSC, give it couple of years dedicated, devoted exclusive time. Just pursue this passion and nothing else. Secondly, I could not do it earlier, because there are severe limitations on a lower middle class family guy like me. We have to start earning as soon as possible because our respective families look up to us. For support. All that matters for this exam is self belief, love for oneself, equanimity and consistency, and most of all, revision, revision and revision.

There is a lot that I want to say, but the space, like us all, has limitations. I hope to see you all in some or the other capacity soon.

MESSAGE TO THE ASPIRANTS

UPSC exam is all about hard work. More than the hard work, its about consistency.

If you do these four things.

❖ have faith in your abilities. if you have faith in you, you'll be rooted and confident about what you are doing, will be confident about your strategy and material and will not get distracted by anything else.

❖ practice a sense of equanimity which means you have to be mentally strong and stable during frustrations the preparation produces.

❖ consistency.

❖ and revision.

If you practice these 4 elements during the course of your preparation. you'll find that even you'll be surprised by how much you can achieve.

❑❑

58

Name: Jyoti Meena
Rank: 741, CSE-2018

Read less, revise more and practice even more, this is the key to success.

JYOTI MEENA

OPTIONAL SUBJECT
Anthropology

MEDIUM
English

NATIVE PLACE
Jaipur

EDUCATIONAL QUALIFICATION
- BTech- MTech, Electrical Engineering, IIT KANPUR

PARENTS' OCCUPATION
- **Father:** Govt. servant, Saras Dairy
- **Mother:** Homemaker

COACHING TAKEN
Followed IAS BABA online initiative only

MY JOURNEY

I have been aspiring for civil service since 2013 and it has been a long time. Hence, I would like to summarise this journey under three headings only.

My Struggle :

- Optimism
- Trust in oneself
- Less is more: read less, revise more and practice even more. Keep it simple.

STUDY PLAN/LIST OF BOOKS

GS

NCERT: 6-12

Laxmikant: Polity

Shankar: Environment

ANTHROPOLOGY

Vivek Bhasme

Brain tree notes

MESSAGE TO NEWCOMERS

- try to prepare own notes and keep updating them (concisely)
- use diagrams and charts wherever possible

IAS BABA test series for prelims

IASBABA/vision IAS for mains

Current affairs from IASBABA DNA (daily news analysis)

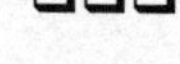